Tall People Don't Jump

Shane Rodgers

Copyright © 2014 Shane Rodgers

All rights reserved.

ISBN: 978-1500207816

For Danielle, Ben and Madeline, who taught me to laugh in all the wrong places.

Thanks to the brilliant Craig Mann for the cover art and to Graeme Wilson for keeping me true to the language. And to all the humans I have ever met – thanks for keeping me amused.

CONTENTS

1. Tall people don't jump

The baffling brain

2. The brain in charge
3. The dreamtime
4. Believing the unbelievable
5. Pursuit of happiness

Curious rituals

6. Doing the time
7. Balloons
8. Jumping castles
9. Changing places
10. The need for speed
11. Waking up
12. Armless intentions
13. Things people do
14. The beach
15. Camping
16. The war against grass
17. Not waving, ironing
18. Cinemas
19. Clapping
20. Opening a jar
21. Wet paint
22. Tying knots
23. Umbrella protocol
24. The spirit of Christmassy

Obsessions

25. Stuff
26. Collecting
27. Because they are there
28. Planet pandemonium
29. Waiting for the windfall

30. Free
31. Apologising to the maid
32. Inferiority complex
33. The weather obsession
34. The mini-bar
35. Smokers
36. Sport – Nature's revenge
37. Computer games
38. Fluff
39. Royalty
40. Going up
41. Turning up
42. Neighbours
43. The thin blue line marker
44. The full inquiry
45. Petrol station protocol
46. Making friends
47. Pedestrian scrambles
48. The other guy
49. The garage
50. Party music
51. Fine print
52. Extras
53. Placed in a queue

Oddities

54. Out of rhyme
55. Kaput
56. Vending machines
57. Passwords
58. Nicknames
59. Beeping
60. Nails on the blackboard
61. Superman syndrome

Getting around

62. Behind the wheel
63. Space invaders
64. Looking like our cars

65. Don't park anywhere
66. Flying high
67. Aircraft lounges

Keeping up appearances

68. Dress code
69. Reflected glory
70. Hats
71. Hair today
72. Male pyjamas

Family life

73. Mating
74. Birth
75. Children
76. Childhood wisdom
77. Passing on wisdom
78. Men as dads
79. Men in hostile territory
80. The plastics cupboard

Consumption

81. Something to chew on
82. Coffee
83. Alcohol

Shopping

84. Shop (till you drop)
85. Lying in wait
86. Taking it back
87. Something smaller
88. Out the back

Animals

89. Whales
90. Dogs

91. A tangled web
92. Insects
93. Fear of vermin
94. Attack from above

Popular culture

95. Too cool
96. The television fixation
97. Rock clips and celebrity interviews
98. Fallen stars
99. Elvis has left the building (sort of)
100. Great trilogies

Politics

101. The curious art of politics
102. American elections
103. The science of spin

Finishing the story

104. The end (almost)

1. Tall people don't jump

Netball is a game that breaks all the rules. At least the players seem to. Pretty much everything you do on a netball court is against the rules. You can't run with the ball, bounce the ball or hold it for more than three seconds. Most parts of the court are out of bounds. If you go there, it is against the rules. If you break the rules, you lose the ball. If you don't break the rules, you still have to get rid of the ball. The only people who are allowed to score goals in netball are a couple of hot shots who they let into the goal circle. Usually these two are the leading goal-scorers when the points are added up at the end of the season. This seems to come as a surprise.

But the rules don't end there. It appears you can't stand too close to people, can't put your hands anywhere that annoys another player, and they don't like you looking at your opponents funny. When you try to block a player, you have to stand like a flamingo and stretch your hands up like a ballerina. This, like most other things, usually results in a penalty.

Netball is mostly played in countries once invaded by Britain and may have emerged from a grand tradition of the British trying to invent new games that they could win. They don't seem to win them anymore and may need to invade some more places to get back their edge. Netball is played in short, pleated skirts that even the umpires often wear. The game will generally accept all-comers, but it is overwhelmingly a girls' sport. The only girls not permitted to play are those with long fingernails. Fingernails are hated by netball umpires across the former British Empire. Arriving at a netball game with long fingernails is one of life's great social faux pas. It can mean instant banishment and shame for the family. Netballers have long known that nothing good ever came from fingernails.

Tall People Don't Jump

I watched my daughters playing netball over countless hours for more than a decade and I still really have no idea what the rules are. All I know is that the whistle will blow approximately every seven seconds, and any player who gets the ball will do exactly nothing with it, before throwing it to another equally hamstrung player. Netball is great for people with a fear of commitment.

But from this game another great lesson has emerged. And it has nothing to do with the rules or the ball. Netball reveals something far deeper and more fundamental about human behaviour and the curious workings of the brain.

You see, both my daughters are vertically challenged, and for the first years they played netball most of the action was happening in the tall-people stratosphere way above their fields of vision. My girls would be running around, trying to look menacing with a flamingo pose when someone was attempting to shoot and generally striving to stay relevant to a game that seemed hopelessly mismatched to their height zone.

I tried to be as encouraging as possible by calling out every few minutes: "Watch your passes." I'm not sure why I called this out, but people who seemed to understand the game were offering the same advice so I'm fairly sure other parents were quite impressed. Sometimes they nodded in agreement and I looked back knowingly.

And then I noticed it...

The giant kids were running around and throwing the ball to each other but that was it. No matter how high the ball went, no matter how many people were after it, no matter how many people yelled out "watch your passes", the feet of these kids almost never left the ground.

Then came the revelation (a drum roll would be handy here): Tall people don't jump.

It was true. If you grow up tall, you don't need to jump. You are already up there all the time. Your brain says (possibly with a superior-sounding European accent): "Do not waste your time jumping, you don't need to." Armed with this information, short people who jump can overcome their natural disadvantage. Their brains are happy to issue the jump order, saying: "Better jump, we're not getting up there any other way."

Suffice to say I encouraged my daughters to jump (and watch their passes and not look at other players funny). They are both fine players who will never play for their country and will break the rules every seven seconds but at least they are in the game. And the tall people have no idea why they don't get the ball every time.

The whole thing got me thinking. If the brain of tall people discourages them from jumping, what other things are our brains doing to us without our knowledge.

This book seeks to find out. It is the culmination of 20 years of observing human beings and plotting their curious behaviour. The results are an intriguing insight into the weird science of the human condition. I'm not sure what the human condition is, but it does not appear to be serious. This book finally exposes the rogue behaviour of the human brain and turns a light on some dark places, as well as some that are fairly well lit.

In some cases, there is actual scientific and social evidence to back the claims. Generally, however, this is just a remarkable coincidence.

The baffling brain

2. The brain in charge

The big problem with the brain is that it is constantly fighting with the rest of the body for control. The brain is a bit like that annoying do-gooder at school who constantly told you why you shouldn't do things. This person generally had short hair, glasses and designer braces, and carried a handkerchief with an initial in the corner. You mostly wanted to hit them. "Don't go there," they would say. "Don't do that or you'll get in trouble." "That's really dangerous."

That is pretty much what the brain does too. It is constantly over-riding our self-conscious plans and deciding something is not worth doing. This is quite deliberate. The brain was built to protect us and prioritise our tasks. It saves the neuron power for something really important like fleeing tigers or escaping fires. It craves novelty and will not waste scarce capacity on things it regards as trivial. As a result, small bits of information are always slipping out of our memory. For example, written text generally has to be read by many people to ensure spelling errors or grammatical mistakes are picked up. A single brain cannot achieve this. Once it has read the same text once, if you try to read it again it will not give it the same priority, and each subsequent read becomes less effective. This is the brain telling you to "talk to the hand" and tell it something it doesn't already know.

A similar problem exists with trying to learn things. It is difficult to remember things just by reading them out of a book. To fully activate your brain you need to trick it into firing up the neurons and freeing up some memory capacity. This requires particularly special study techniques like memorising things while you are being chased by a tiger.

It appears the brain, with its 100 billion or so cells, has been hard-wired over many centuries of genetic evolution to help you do the right thing. While there has been debate for centuries about whether a sense of right or wrong is learnt or innate, there is certainly plenty of credible evidence that at least some of our basic sense of piety is in our genetics.

Whenever we are tempted to do something we know is wrong, the core operations centre of the brain fires off a warning, like "swim between the flags" or "don't go out drinking". Quite often you go out drinking anyway. In the morning, the brain extracts its revenge by waking you up early and giving you a headache, thus proving the brain is a bastard. Sometimes you try to punish it by swimming outside the flags. This often results in death and is not recommended.

It is difficult to tell just how much we can actually upload into an average human brain. Former Australian of the Year Fiona Stanley often uses slide pictures showing neuron pathways in a newborn, a toddler and a teenager. These slides reveal that we are born with scant brain activity, but within a few years our head is a spaghetti junction of active neurons waiting for us to send in the knowledge. The brain obviously gets tired of waiting, and by our teens many of the pathways have been shut down and de-wired. We grow up being told we use only about 10 per cent of our brain. Yet the brain control centre still refuses to be generous with the available space and help us remember everything we want. As a result, most of us end up feeling like Homer Simpson, who laments that every time he remembers something it pushes something else out of his brain.

It also seems likely that the brain has a sense of humour. How often, for example, do we get asked a question and know it is "on the tip of our tongue". Clearly this is the brain having a bit of fun and holding back the answer. Alternatively, this particular bit of information may be stored in some rusted old neurone filing cabinet in an obscure part of your brain and it is taking your brain-control cells a little while to put on their glasses and find it.

The situation is even worse when you are trying to remember somebody's name. They are walking towards you and you are thinking: "I know this person, brain please send me the name". Suddenly in your head, the brain-control cells are pulling out old pictures from barely-used files, trying to match them with a name. Inevitably you come up short and have to greet the person with a: "How are YOU going?" The person knows straight away that you can't remember their name but seldom gets insulted because usually they have forgotten yours too. Of course, if you meet this person again any time soon, you will remember their name for sure. The trauma of an embarrassing name-loss incident sends your brain into crisis mode and that file is restored to a more accessible place for the future. In some cases it even goes under the brain's equivalent of a fridge magnet with all the other must-remembers. That is unless you get the dreaded "mental block". This is when the file is there but nobody knows where to find it. This is no fun. Nothing good ever came from a mental block.

Of course, there are really intelligent people who seem to remember everything. They have apparently been blessed with a head full of anal-retentive nerd neurones that go around tidying things up and actually know how the brain's filing system works. People with brains like this ultimately end up on quiz shows knowing the floral emblem of Tunisia and how to spell the names of cities in former Soviet republics. These people usually win the car and the holiday, as well as lots of cash they will ultimately lose in an investment scheme that looked too good to be true.

Other quiz-show participants have camera-shy neurones that stare, stunned bunny-style, into the camera when the stage lights go on, or have slow and measured neurones that know the answer but can't get a signal to the hand to push the buzzer. In these cases the human who is on television is left looking like a nong and goes home with a useless piece of specially-crafted jewellery and an equally unnecessary kitchen appliance they bought in the gift shop.

Of course, when this happens, there is not a whole lot you can do to seek retribution from the brain. It knows what you are thinking and is therefore hard to control and punish. As soon as you start to think anything negative about your brain, the neurone fire brigade comes along and extinguishes the thought. In political terms, the brain is the undisputed dictator of your body. It commands the other organs and dictates the terms. To a point. The heart and lungs also have a fair bit of clout because, even if they went on a short strike, half the brain's neurones would shut down. But the evidence is overwhelming. It is time the brain was brought to account and made to pull its weight ... hang on, what was I talking about?

3. The dreamtime

If we require further evidence of the rogue behaviour of our brains, we need look no further than dreams. When we sleep, it is as if all our experiences of the day are mangled up with all the experiences of our lives and compiled into an oddly-edited Quentin Tarantino film. While we are dreaming it seems to make perfect sense that we are driving our cars in water, with our Grade 10 English teacher in the back, solving a Scooby-Doo style mystery involving the person we had a meeting with this morning to discuss building maintenance. It seems equally plausible that at some stage during the dream we will be chased by the kid who bullied us at school, who will turn out to be the guy at the toll booth who is actually Batman.

Tall People Don't Jump

At no stage during the dream process does our brain say: "This whole thing is crazy. What the hell am I doing?" Of course when we wake up we are fairly embarrassed by the whole thing. Luckily no-one else can get inside your head. It is fairly scary in there at times. Sometimes we attempt to describe our dreams to others. This is best avoided. What goes on in the dream should stay in the dream. Some things are just between you and your brain.

The other inevitability of a dream is that in a really good dream you will wake up before you get to the best part. It's like your brain is saying: "Wait for it, wait for it – wake him up NOW." This causes a lot of mirth inside your head by bored neurones who have nothing better to do at night. Sometimes you try to go straight back to sleep in an attempt to restart the dream. This never works. By now the brain is ready to load a totally new tape or put a bad experience at the office right in your prime zone so you can't sleep for the rest of the night.

On the up side, scary dreams also tend to end before you actually die. The brain is fairly squeamish in this regard. It is happy to have you hanging off a cliff, being trapped by rising water, or at the mercy of a crazed toll-booth employee. But it lets you off the hook before it goes too far. Often this is not before it has woken up all the adrenalin cells, activated the sweat cells and generally set off all the body's fire alarms. When you wake up from a bad dream there is no rush to go back to sleep. You hope the brain will put a bad experience at the office in your prime zone so you don't have to go back to the cliff.

My theory on all this is that during the day the brain cell A-team is on deck, generally responding quickly to messages from the nervous system and the eyes, ears and nose, and providing useful and timely mind images. At night the A-team is off-duty and the B-team takes over. This team is not very good. They do not really know how to work the equipment and tend to get the files mixed up or play the wrong tapes. Often the B-team will play the same dream several times over months and years. This is either because they are too lazy to make new ones, or some of them have called in sick and they make the decision to screen repeats. The night neurones don't really enjoy their work and the care factor is generally zero. Most of them resent the A-team and are quite happy to deprive you of deep sleep and mind harmony just to annoy the arrogant upstarts who run the body during the day. You can imagine the A-team coming in first thing in the morning and finding the control room full of pizza, the files all over the shop and a body that will only function with a burst of caffeine.

There is a line in the song *Where the river meets the sea* that says: "What a newborn baby dreams is a mystery." This is very interesting. Baby dreams can't be all that compelling – there is so little material to work with and their lives at that point are mostly about breast milk and poop. This might explain why babies wake up every four hours. We have generally assumed that this is because they are hungry. In fact, it could be that their heads have run out of dreams and the B-team has sent out an all-points-bulletin seeking new material.

Of course, dreams are not always a waste of time. Over time the word "dream" has also come to be associated with hopes and aspirations. Many of the world's great minds claim to have received inspiration from dreams. Albert Einstein traced the origins of his Theory of Relativity to a boyhood dream about a sled ride. American inventor Elias Howe is said to have perfected the Singer sewing machine after a dream about cannibals with holes in the points of their spears. Paul McCartney, from The Beatles, was delivered the melody for *Yesterday* in a dream. It took him quite a while to convince himself that he hadn't inadvertently swiped it from someone else. The 1936 medicine and physiology Nobel Prize winner Otto Leowi said he dreamt the experiment that led to the discovery of chemical neurotransmitters. That must have been one exciting dream. Perhaps in these instances the brain's A-team are insomniacs, or prefer to work nights for social reasons. Dreams in the hands of professionals are obviously a far more important incubator of creative thought than the B-grade mind flicks most of us put up with.

Naturally, when we have bad dreams or repeat dreams we look for meaning in them. This is where professional dream interpreters come in. The dream almost always has a meaning vastly unlike what you expected. For example, if we have a near miss with a car in traffic during the day, all night we are likely to dream about almost running into things. We automatically assume this means we have had a near miss and are worried about running into things. This is wrong. The experts are more likely to tell us it actually means we have a fear of attachment or we feel our lives are a constant battle to avoid the things we don't want to face up to. Generally our parents are to blame for this, or possibly the government.

Of course, the other dream theory is that our conscious mind is very pragmatic and businesslike, like Agent Gibbs in NCIS. During the day, when the body needs to be active, deal quickly with problems and avoid running into things, it needs to perform like a military operation. It must be rational and efficient. At night, all the arty parts of the brain, which are not allowed out when you are active in case they break something, are let loose on the mind. This group do role play, experiment with abstract concepts and do experiments on parts of your brain that are usually dormant. Sometimes they play dress-ups. While the average person has about five dreams during a normal night's sleep, they tend not to remember many of them. This is usually a good thing. In fact, I suspect the arty neurone group are embarrassed by some of their work and deliberately erase the memory, delete the temporary files and clear the history.

Another interesting possibility is the link between dreams and déjà vu. Most people have incidents in their lives that seem to be an exact repeat of something that has happened before. Sometimes they appear to be living something they previously dreamt. If you believe in déjà vu, this suggests the brain has some sort of psychic qualities that allow it to predict the future. If this is true, you have to wonder why it uses this amazing power to predict generally mundane encounters and conversations but fails to deliver you the Lotto numbers.

4. Believing the unbelievable

Despite all the apparent firepower in our brain cells, humans still have a remarkable capacity to believe things that, on any objective analysis, seem unbelievable. There is always a percentage who will invest in financial schemes that are obviously too good to be true, answer emails from Nigeria asking for their bank details, and believe that women will obey their husbands because they said so in the wedding vows.

Every mad cult seems to find people who believe a spaceship will take them away to a better place, and there are always individuals who will give all their possessions to a pseudo-religious guru with a book and a charismatic tone. In some respects this is no surprise. Although people seldom talk about it, many are uneasy about their mortality and spirituality and vulnerable to people who seem to have answers that might protect them and give them meaning and purpose. They also seem prone to cheap deals on roof painting.

In fact, if a reasonable-sounding person says almost anything with enough conviction, a certain proportion of people will accept it as "scientific fact" and relate the story to others with equal conviction. This results in dozens of popular myths, thousands of websites, and untold conspiracy theories. Thousands of people, for example, still question whether man actually walked on the moon, even though the conspiracy to fake this would have been much more technically difficult than landing a glorified tin can on a giant rock. Equally, for years there was a strong belief that entertainer Elvis Presley had faked his death in 1977 to escape the spotlight. He was subsequently "spotted" everywhere from Mexico to the late-night supermarket and hamburger joints.

There are a lot of theories on why people believe apparently unbelievable things. One is that they are bonkers. If this is true, however, there are many millions of bonkers people walking around. This seems too hard to believe, even for the human brain. Another theory is that homo-sapiens have managed to keep an edge in the survival chain over the years by being open to alternative theories, methods and ideas that set us apart from the basic instincts of most animals.

In his book *Why People Believe Weird Things*, Professor Michael Shermer puts strange beliefs down to wishful thinking and unwillingness by people to admit they are wrong. These convictions become so powerful that people will continue to believe them even in the face of compelling contrary evidence. As a result, over time humans have burnt "witches" at the stake, denied major historical events ever happened, and swore they were cured by some snake oil they bought from a guy with a loud voice on the back of a truck.

Shermer says that to justify a "weird" position, people tend to concentrate on opponents' weak points and errors made by protagonists rather than the core argument on the existence of something unusual. They focus on what is not known rather than what is known. In this context, he points out that just because something cannot be explained with a rational explanation now, doesn't mean there isn't one. Magic tricks, for example, generally look impossible to the untrained eye. For people who know how they work, the illusion is just that. Imagine what a 17th century man would have thought of a TV remote control. The electrical salesman might also have been burnt at the stake.

As with the snake oil, it is also easy to put two totally unrelated things together and rationalise that one is the result of another. This is particularly true with superstitions. People might have a run of luck at the casino when they have a lucky charm around their neck or they are wearing their "lucky shirt". However, there is every chance their luck would have been just as good if they had neither.

Curiously, believing apparently strange things is not limited to the intellectually challenged or the uneducated. Part of the reason unusual theories and beliefs attract broad followings is because highly intelligent people often espouse them. Shermer has some thoughts on this too. He believes smart people become very skilled at defending viewpoints they arrived at for non-smart reasons. Core beliefs are also a product of a variety of factors that go beyond logic and evidence, such as genetic predispositions, parent, sibling and peer influence and social and cultural factors.

Unusual beliefs can result from the void created when science and rational thought do not yet have a viable explanation. For example, until Christopher Columbus circled the globe, there was a general acceptance even among the intellectual classes that the world was flat. I am not sure what they thought happened to all the water that poured over the side or where the water came from to replace it, but if enough reasonable-sounding people believe it, theories can quickly become fact. What's more, people with alternative views or theories were often beguiled or written off as quacks. The father of modern astronomy, Galileo Galilei, copped a pounding and was accused of heresy because he did not believe the earth was the centre of the universe. Of course, in modern times we now know that Kim Kardashian, Paris

Hilton and Lindsay Lohan are, in fact, the centre of the universe.

There is a famous Australian internet company commercial in which a young boy asks his father why the Great Wall of China was built. The father, who has no idea, explains that it was built during the reign of emperor Nasi Goreng to keep the rabbits out. Not only did the advertisement highlight how gullible we are to false information that sounds rational, it will almost certainly result in thousands of Australian children believing that the Chinese wall is, in fact, the most extravagant rabbit–proof fence ever conceived. Australian tourists in China now notoriously ask the guides at the Great Wall if it was built to keep the rabbits out of China. This started as a joke but over time it may well enter into folklore and be repeated in the future as a fact.

This would not be the first time that the Great Wall had been the subject of a truism that may have no basis in fact. Almost everyone knows, for example, that the Great Wall of China is the only man-made structure that can be seen from space. But can it really be seen from space? Perhaps from Google Earth but there seems to be great doubts that an astronaut gazing out the window from a spacecraft can actually see it. In fact, a Chinese space mission in 2004 was fairly adamant that the wall, albeit great, was simply not visible from space.

There are many other examples. The first President of the United States, George Washington, is widely reputed to have had wooden false teeth and to have chopped down an apple tree (or perhaps a cherry tree) when he was a child and owned up to it straight away because he could not tell a lie. It now seems widely accepted that neither of these stories is actually true.

In the 1990s many people at dinner parties recounted the story of a Japanese fishing boat that was sunk when it was hit by a cow falling from the sky. The story went that the cow was stolen by some Russian soldiers who shoved it out the rear of a plane when it became restless during the flight. In some versions of the story there are multiple cows and boats, or the cow falls onto cars rather than fishing boats. This tale apparently started as a joke but got veracity when a German newspaper reported it as fact. As a result, it is still recounted as fact, often on apparently credible websites and in mainstream publications. It is such a good story that people want to believe it is true.

UFO sightings are another example. There have been thousands of these, often by normal, well-adjusted people with little vested interest in manufacturing a story. Many sightings are written off as weather balloons. This is equally strange. I'm not sure there are even such things as weather balloons. They sound important but do weather forecasters really have a whole lot of balloons floating around the sky all the time? I suspect they are just as rare as extra-terrestrial craft. Some people swear they have been abducted by aliens and subjected to experiments. These experiments usually seem to involve anal probes. It is not clear why aliens are so interested in human anuses. Perhaps this is the most advanced form of our anatomy and we have just taken it for granted over all of these years. Governments are generally accused of knowing about the existence of aliens but keeping it a secret. This is to avoid panic, and out of a general respect for the whole anal area.

Crop circles were for years seen as definitive proof of alien landings. How else could circles be formed in corn fields with no trail leading there or leading away? As it turns out, a couple of guys and a rope can do the same thing. In 1991 two Englishmen admitted to creating hundreds of these circles. There are plenty of others they didn't create, but the alien theory is looking increasingly doubtful.

People regularly report sightings of monsters like the Yowie and the Yeti, but there is seldom real evidence to support the sightings. After his death, it was revealed that the man behind much of the Bigfoot "evidence", Ray Wallace, had faked all of it as a joke. Similarly, another near-to-death-bed confession revealed the most famous photograph of Scotland's Loch Ness monster was also a fake. In fact it was a deliberate hoax using a toy submarine. Deep down, people want to believe the existence of extraordinary things. Generally, however, they prove to be quite explainable.

The ability of the brain to believe in some fairly far-fetched concepts begins in childhood when parents conspire to convince their offspring that Santa Claus, the Easter Bunny and the Tooth Fairy are real. Someone once observed that men go through three stages in their lives: they believe in Santa Claus; they don't believe in Santa Claus; they are Santa Claus. As a result, between the ages of about two and 10, humans are capable of accepting that a fat guy in an impractical suit comes down the chimney and delivers presents to every child in the world on a single night in December. They accept that this occurs in a flying sleigh pulled by reindeer and that this can all be achieved while consuming several billion cookies and millions of litres of milk. The toys he brings are produced at the North Pole, for reasons that are never completely clear, and the whole thing is organised around lists that are checked twice to ascertain who has been ill-disciplined and who has been pleasant. In some versions of the story, the wayward get no presents, or a bag of coal. Santa Claus is always strangely jolly despite his workload and bleak geographical locale. He almost certainly has a drinking problem, but they don't mention this in the kids' books.

There seem to be few theories on how the Easter Bunny actually gets into the house. Children are taught stranger danger from a young age, but nobody questions a giant rabbit being in the house in the middle of the night, eating the vegetables and leaving candy for the youngsters. If children really analysed the whole Bunny caper, they would be totally freaked out. They trust their parents enough to go along with it. And throughout their lives the Easter experience teaches them to trust anyone who brings chocolate.

Logic is stretched even further with the Tooth Fairy. The theory goes that when you lose a tooth, a fairy enters your room and replaces it with a coin. It is never entirely clear what the fairies do with the teeth or why they are flying around with coins. Of course, if kids were smart they would hoard the teeth in a kind of tooth futures market and put them all out in the future when inflation dictates a better coin, or even a note.

5. The pursuit of happiness

Human beings have grown up believing that they should be happy. In fact, most people consider it a right. Sometimes they will sit around waiting for it to happen. "Any moment now I will feel happy," they think. This almost never works. Like most good things, happiness tends to only appear if you don't see it coming.

Conventional wisdom is that we can only achieve "true" happiness from non-material things. Following this logic, if material things make us happy, this is not "true" happiness. Nobody seems to be able to tell the difference, but we avoid arguing with this type of reason, particularly if the person making the claim sounds like they know what they are talking about, or have a regular spot on afternoon television. This causes people to constantly ask themselves if they are "truly" happy. For all we know we are actually all miserable, but we don't have any yardsticks for comparison except for people in evangelistic churches who all seem to be happy, sometimes creepily so.

A powerful undertone of this conventional wisdom is that money is not necessary for happiness. I remember reading the following bit of wisdom in a *Cracked* magazine when I was a kid: "Money can't buy happiness but it makes misery a lot more fun."

It is hard to argue with this logic. Most rich people indeed seem to enjoy quality misery as they frolic on their yachts, go to interesting places and have great food served to them. You've got to feel sorry for those poor bastards.

The other conventional wisdom on happiness comes from the famous passage by Souza:

> "For a long time it seemed to me that life was about to begin – real life. But there was always some obstacle in the way, something to be gotten through first, some unfinished business, time still to be served, a debt to be paid. At last it dawned on me that these obstacles were my life. This perspective has helped me to see there is no way to happiness. Happiness is the way. So treasure every moment you have and remember that time waits for no one. Happiness is a journey, not a destination."

This is, of course, quite depressing and hopefully bunkum. It does, however, fit very well on coffee mugs and fridge magnets. If happiness is a journey, no wonder so many people are so miserable. If we follow this logic, when we go on long trips with children and they ask if we are there yet, we should say: "We're not going anywhere, it's all about the journey." That would work. We should have just gone to the moon, not actually landed on it. And athletes who come last but make the distance should be just as happy as those who win the medals.

Modern humans are a bit obsessed with journeys. It seems that most of them are on a journey to "discover" themselves. On reality shows, particularly any that involve singing and dancing, everyone talks about their journey. The judges, the audience, the public and most members of their families have come with them on a journey. Some have spent hundreds of dollars voting for them with text messages. This keeps them happy until their person gets evicted. Then they get their phone bill and feel ripped off because all their votes did was make television companies richer. Eventually they accept this as part of their personal journey.

Some businesses try to capitalise on the human pursuit of happiness by introducing concepts like "happy hour". Happy hour at hotels generally involves cheap alcohol. Alcohol-induced happiness is also frowned on because it is seldom still there when you wake up, and sometimes your head hurts a lot. But it is hard to knock them for trying. If half-price beer makes just one person's life better, then happy hour probably should be encouraged.

Happiness is a popular theme in songs, particularly bad songs sung by twee, middle-of-the-road performers who smile too much. Sometimes people refer to psychiatric facilities as "happy farms". I'm not sure if anyone buys this. These people are mostly not happy, and there is little evidence of crops or barnyard animals. John Lennon sang that happiness was a warm gun. Later he was shot dead. This suggests he was probably wrong.

Curious rituals

6. Doing the time

At some point in the evolution of human history, someone with too much daylight on their hands decided it would be a good idea to measure time. Measured time is a totally artificial creation. Our cave people ancestors were fairly content with night and day. Now we must measure every millisecond and arrive everywhere at precisely the right moment.

Time is generally based on how long it takes the earth to rotate once (a day), how long it takes for the moon to orbit the earth (a month), how long it takes for the earth to orbit the sun (a year) and how long it takes to negotiate peak hour traffic (forever). Even this is not entirely precise. At midnight on New Year's Eve

2008, the custodians of time had to add an extra second to all the clocks because the earth had slowed down. We probably did not notice the extra second too much, but in a time-poor world, we are happy to take anything extra that comes along. We might even save it up for when we are running a few seconds late.

The invention of time spawned an unexpected human obsession – the anniversary. Over many centuries, the human race has developed an obsession with the length of time people do things. As a result, the media is full of stories celebrating people, organisations or companies that have been doing something for a long time. These must be celebrated annually, every five years, 10 years, years that divide by four, 20 years, 21 years, 30 years and so on. Anniversaries of any type are usually celebrated with cake and speeches. People feel proud that they have reached this milestone. Sometimes there are even festive hats.

The anniversary obsession results in many stories in the media giving us great insight into the subject of the celebrations. There are stories that tell us that Bill has worked in the same job for 30 years. "Thirty years?" people say. "That sure is a lot of years, a heck of a lot of years." Then there is the whitegoods company that has "been around" for 45 years and not gone broke. "Forty-five years!" people say. "That sure is a lot of years to be around, a whole lot of years."

Anniversaries are usually accompanied by compelling historical evidence to verify the length of time involved. This is often a black and white photograph of some strangely-dressed people in front of a sign. These people generally wear hats and trousers that are worn just below the armpit (the trousers, not the hats). The people look very funny, but it is generally considered disrespectful to laugh at them, particularly if one of them has turned up for the anniversary wearing their trousers just under their armpits.

The most prominent of all anniversaries is the human birthday.

All humans have one each year, but everyone still seems amazed by them. Whole workplaces will stop to celebrate a birthday. In firms of several hundred people, there is pretty much a birthday or two every day. This results in a lot of cake and quite a bit of obesity. The birthday creates particular challenges for the people giving the birthday speeches. They are effectively celebrating the fact that someone has made it through another year. Not a lot of material there. Thankfully, speech-makers can always make a joke about eating too much cake or drinking too much alcohol. All brains are pre-wired to laugh at anything that involves excessive cake or alcohol. This special brain function has been saving birthday speeches for as long as history has been recorded.

The most complex birthday celebrations involve young children, who expect a memorable celebration because they are kids and don't know any better, and they have had so few birthdays that they still seem important. Children's birthday parties generally resemble the annual running of the bulls, but with slightly more carnage. Children up until the age of about eight simply run around and scream at birthday parties. They stop briefly to consume food with no apparent nutritional value (another birthday staple) and then resume their running and screaming. Sometimes a clown arrives to entertain the children. The clown usually gets poked a lot and kicked in the groin. On bad days his fake nose will be ripped off and plonked in the punch. Parents dread children's birthday parties all year. They are three hours of hell, followed by five hours of cleaning when you inevitably find doughnuts in the DVD player, and the family cat tied up to the clothes line. The whole thing is generally recorded and stored in a special drawer, never to be played again.

The ultimate anniversary involves a century (100 years). Anyone or anything that has been around for 100 years must be celebrated with Defcon 5 intensity. When a person turns 100, the Queen gets so astounded she sends them a telegram. This is despite telegrams not even existing any more. There are special clubs for people who have reached 100, and any company or organisation that is still around for 100 years is considered very lucky, or government-subsidised.

Of course, no story about someone doing something (like living) for a lot of years is complete without a secret. "What is the secret for doing that all those years?" someone will ask. "Nothing much," is the usual reply. "Nothing much, is it?" people will think. "Now that's some advice worth keeping. I too will do nothing much." A lot of people who turn 100 claim to have done so by breaking all the rules – smoking, drinking and eating lots of meat. Others credit "good living". Nobody is really sure what good living is, but it apparently involves broccoli and plenty of roughage.

Older people celebrating anniversaries also like to recount things that happened a long time ago. This is generally because they have quality memories of the past, but many of them in later years forget to put their teeth in. In particular, older people like to remember the price of things. "When I was a boy," they say, "you could buy ice-cream for twopence at Mr Hooper's store, and bread was 5 cents. Five of us used to ride a donkey for two hours through floodwater to get to school, and we lived on bread and dripping." People are very astounded by these recollections. "I'm not sure what twopence is," they think, "but it does sound very cheap for an ice-cream. This is quite astounding." People are also secretly thankful that they did not ride a donkey to school with four others through floodwater. "That sounds fairly uncomfortable," they think. "I think this person may have made the whole thing up."

Of course, with so many of them happening, people always struggle to find ways to celebrate an anniversary. With marriages, milestone years are marked with different types of stones. This is apparently the result of a conspiracy between women and jewellery stores to keep men broke and under pressure to deliver increasingly-larger precious rocks. The practice is a big contributor to the chronic divorce rate, as men succumb to the pressure and bail out while they are still in the cheap rock range.

Anniversaries in the workplace are generally celebrated with watches for men and some type of vase or kitchen glass-setting combo for women. In some companies there are plaques which declare the person involved has indeed been around for a long time. These plaques usually get pride of place on the wall so everyone can marvel at the wonder of passing time.

7. Balloons

Most aspects of modern society would fail to function effectively without balloons. Balloons are used to reflect mood, character, celebration and end-of-model run-out sales. Balloons on a letterbox are an internationally recognised symbol that a children's party is in progress. During wartime, nobody bombs a building with a red cross or balloons. They figure those parents have been through enough already. And chances are the children have already done more damage than could be inflicted by a bomb.

It is extremely difficult to effectively take part in western society without the ability to inflate a balloon. In modern times this can be achieved with gas or a pump. A pump is generally considered cheating if you have fewer than 500 balloons to inflate. Traditionally they had to be inflated using your actual mouth. Manual balloon inflation has two stages – the initial air thrust booster and the full-inflation continuous blow-out. Generally the initial air thrust booster is the most difficult part. If you can't get the balloon started, you look like a complete goose. Your face also goes very red and, on a bad day, you hyperventilate.

Reaching the air thrust booster point takes undying confidence in the ability of your lungs. Some people never really master it.

Others fail to trap the air once they reach initial inflation, allowing it to backflow at pace into their mouths and pump out their cheeks. This is always funny until someone loses a lung.

The full-inflation continuous blow-out is relatively simple because, by the time you have reached this point, the balloon has realised that resistance is futile. It is resigned to becoming obese, and vulnerable to a pin or equally sharp object. The biggest difficulty with the final balloon inflation is knowing when to stop. There is no commonly-acceptable standard for the right size for an inflated balloon. And the only real way to know you have gone too far is when it blows up in your face. This is never good. It is almost impossible to look cool when a balloon has just blown up in your face.

While balloons are not actual living things, when inflated they seem to develop a sense of empathy and camaraderie. If one balloon bursts, all the others seem to also burst in a type of giant balloon mass suicide. This generally causes people to jump, because bursting balloons sound a bit like gunfire, except a bit more rubbery.

The obsession with balloons has extended to the creation of giant balloons that float around in the sky carrying humans in a little cane Easter basket underneath. Giant balloons are also used in big parades, and as corporate promotion vehicles that sometimes float over football fields and film the action from too far away to see it.

Balloons can either contain ordinary human air or a gas called helium. Helium allows the balloons to float into the air. It also causes the human voice to sound like a chipmunk. This provides a guaranteed laugh. Humans talking like chipmunks are always funny.

At almost any celebratory human activity, children are provided with balloons. Despite this being a fairly common event, most children are incapable of actually holding on to their balloon for more than about five minutes. When they let go of balloons without helium, the father can generally chase these down across the paddock as the wind toys with him and keeps pushing them out of reach. Helium balloons are a different story. An escaped helium balloon will head straight into the sky. Fathers will always try to jump up and catch them, but they are nearly always unsuccessful and mostly end up looking like idiots. This is generally the first time that a child sees his or her father failing miserably. This comes as a big disappointment.

8. Jumping castles

The jumping castle is the most poignant symbol of western civilisation. When future historians study the 20th and 21st centuries, they will devote significant chapters to the dark mysteries of the castle full of air. Biologists will use the jumping castles as a prime example of what separates humans from other animals. "Ants and cockroaches may be tough and strong," they will say, "but where are their jumping castles?"

The jumping castle is also symbolic of a civilisation at the height of its progress. During the Dark Ages and the Russian Revolution, there were very few jumping castles. In fact, throughout history humans have built many castles, but it took many centuries for them to be jumping. This is a great shame. The Dark Ages, for example, would have been a lot more fun with a few jumping castles.

For modern children, the jumping castle is the difference between a non-event and a must-go activity. When parents are trying to entice them to go places, the inevitable question arises: "Mummy will there be a jumping castle?" If the answer is "yes", they are in the car within seconds.

Part of the appeal of the jumping castle is that it allows children to do all the things they can't do at home. It is just like jumping on your parents' bed (which is always funny until someone falls out the window), but you can make all the noise you want and nobody ever sends you to bed.

Child psychoanalytical types fear many parents are using the jumping castle as a baby-sitter and substitute for valuable family time. They fear that the children do not learn much from the jumping castle. They just jump up and down. Apparently nobody ever learnt much from jumping up and down.

But that is what makes the jumping castle so special. Its reason for being is bedded deep in the psyche of the human condition: "I jump, therefore I am."

9. Changing places

Moving house is one of the most stressful things you can do. Psychologists put it in the same league as losing a close relative, having a baby, and waiting for the eviction announcement on Master Chef.

Moving involves taking all your worldly possessions, putting them in a pile, and then making an even three-way carve-up between the local tip, the packing boxes and the charity bins. Moving is performed by large men in vans who must take your giant furniture out through tiny doors without scratching or denting it. Sometimes they drop your washing machine by accident. Washing machines are never the same again after a move. They are a non-nomadic appliance.

Long before you get to this stage, you must acquire the packing boxes. This is never easy. You can, of course, just buy them – but most humans, particularly men, have a philosophical objection to paying for cardboard boxes. Our instincts tell us that the world has so many boxes they really should be free, like content on the internet.

During one of my family's moves, we took on the job of box-collecting as a joint family initiative. Wherever we went, we were on the lookout for them. First I tried a major fast-food company which sells thousands of fries and burgers every day which must come out of boxes. This had to be the box El Dorado – the magical place box-hunters everywhere whisper about in hushed tones. I phoned and they were very co-operative. "Boxes," they said, "of course we have boxes. Will there be any fries with those?"

The next day, as arranged, I arrived at the local outlet, rolled up to the counter and said I was there for the boxes. This was clearly an unusual request. Before you could say "eat here or take away" the manager was called. He explained that they did have boxes, but something had gone seriously awry with the whole box plan. He'd left instructions for the night workers to leave the boxes but, alas, there were now no boxes. It seems their training programme included a ritual of "breaking down" the boxes as they were unpacked. Once they were trained, it was extremely difficult to break the habit. And once a box was broken down, it was a goner. No box has ever returned from a solid breaking down.

Undaunted, the manager assured me if I came back the next day there would be lots of boxes. I was reassured by this and, so no-one would think I was the sort of person who would just rock up, take the boxes and drive off without even a 30 cent cone, I ordered a Coke and a small burger, noting that neither came in a box.

I came the next day with the trailer in anticipation of a successful box-hunting day. The manager saw me and I knew right away something had gone terribly wrong. The oasis that was my boxes had become but a desert of cheese burgers and quarter-pounders. It seemed that once these workers were trained to break down boxes, the process could never be reversed. I was dealing with the unboxables.

It was time to try a new strategy. For a few days we went to one of those supermarkets that still lets you have your groceries in a box. We bought tiny grocery orders and brought them home in gigantic boxes. As moving day approached, barely half our stuff was packed and the box supply was rapidly dwindling. At this point Operation Box-hunt moved to code red. We needed a miracle. And it came in the guise of banana guy.

It was a chance meeting. We happened to be at the supermarket buying things we actually needed when we asked if there might be some boxes around for enthusiastic, but humble, box-hunters such as ourselves. We had come to the right place. The woman had dealt with our kind before and she gave us a knowing, secret smile. "You want boxes, she said, "you talk to the banana guy."

The banana guy was young, but his face somehow showed a wisdom beyond his years. "You've come for the boxes, haven't you grasshopper?" he asked. (I don't think he actually called me grasshopper, but my brain has since added that bit to give my memory a hint of the martial arts guru from Kung Fu. I am okay with this). "Come back in two hours," the banana guy said. "I'll see what I can do for you."

Two hours later I returned without high hopes, still reeling from the fast-food outlet experience. I'm not sure what happened in those two hours, but when we returned a pile of banana boxes was standing like an oracle before us in the fading afternoon light. As we carried them to the trailer, we noticed the admiring stares of others in the car park. "Those people have a lot of boxes," a middle-aged couple was overheard to exclaim. It was true. We did have a lot of boxes, a hell of a lot of boxes. We had fulfilled the dream of all house-movers. It was a day of great pride.

In the hours and days that followed, we packed all our worldly goods into these boxes with great care. The boxes protected our things and saw them safely on the long journey to the new home. We had broken the box break-down bogey. Unfortunately, however, everything we own now smells of bananas.

10. The need for speed

In recent years there has been something of an obsession with young people who are loosely referred to as Generation Y (Gen Y for short or in text messaging). Older people treat Gen Y as if they are an alien species, and often talk about them as if they are not there. Sometimes they prod them to see if they will react.

All generations are "different". Gen Y is completely different, having grown up in an era when the internet is a natural extension of their brains – a group described by media magnate Rupert Murdoch as "digital natives".

There are many things that set Gen Y apart – they are global thinkers, oozing with self-belief, demanding, tech-savvy and unimpressed by much. They appear to have pretty much no attention span and they say "whatever" a lot ("What part of whatever don't you understand?"). But the thing that really sets them apart is the speed with which they do things.

They text fast, walk fast, change channels every 14.5 seconds, can't wait for the lift, and type emails as if they are diffusing a bomb. The exception to this speed fetish is the department store checkout. These checkouts are inhabited almost entirely by Gen Y people, yet the males in particular scan the items as if they are in slow-motion replay. The speed does not change no matter how long the waiting line is, and store policy prevents you speeding them up by whacking them a few times with a colourful, inflatable baseball bat. This is known as the Gen Y paradox and might also explain why the French drink a lot.

Gen Y reportedly consumes four different types of media before 8am each day (on the occasions when they are awake by then) and they have no tolerance for things that don't work. They have somehow rewired their brains to allow them to do homework while watching television, listening to an iPod and texting their friends.

Hyper-drive young people appear to be a by-product of a world with too many options to fit into a single 24-hour period. This is a modern plague that besets all western civilisations and generations. As a result, everyone wastes a lot of time bemoaning how little time they have, how quickly the year has gone, how rapidly their life is passing them by and how much caffeine they are forced to consume to keep up with it all.

Most people seem to have worked out that the only way to do everything they think they need to do in a day is to rush a lot. Hence, peak transits have become known as rush hours, takeaways are fast food, highways have come to resemble Indy race tracks, and if you don't keep moving on a big-city footpath, you just get trampled to death. People are in a rush to get to work, a rush to get home, a rush to get lunch before their time is up, and constantly on deadlines that must be met, or else.

Yet, despite all the options, humans are also doing individual things for longer, particularly working. Americans in the 21st century apparently work more hours than peasants did in the Middle Ages and spend less time on leisure. High proportions of people across the western world fail to take their allotted annual leave (too busy to stop), and leisure that technology once promised has generally failed to eventuate.

Children have been sucked into the save time-speed vortex. According to a study by the University of Michigan's Survey Research Center, since the late 1970s children have lost 12 hours of free time each week. This includes a 25 per cent drop in play time and a 50 per cent drop in unstructured outdoor activities.

Much of the time has been taken up in homework, which had doubled during that period and even actual time at school.

This trend has undoubtedly necessitated an astonishing increase in the types and volume of homework excuses. Few teachers today believe that goldfish actually eat homework. You are better off saying that time pressures put you into total meltdown and you needed therapy, possibly retail. Everyone will believe that.

Time poverty has manifested itself in other ways. People are sleeping less. According to Mark Penn's *Microtrends,* the average American now sleeps less than seven hours a night, and 16 per cent sleep fewer than six hours. This results in a lot of sleepy people, and has helped fuel the coffee boom that is helping to keep most of the western world awake all day. Sleeping less hurts productivity and contributes to obesity. By 3pm, large numbers of people are starting to "fade" and might even fall asleep at their desks.

Time starvation has robbed society of discretionary time that people previously used for volunteering and community engagement. As a result, many organisations are starved for members, and a lot of community support has collapsed. This was outlined in great detail in Robert Putnam's *Bowling Alone*. The trend is also hurting the environment. We don't have time to wash up, and we need to eat quickly so we buy pre-packaged food, produced quickly in manic kitchens on disposable plates. We grab it, we use it, we get rid of it – no time to mess around.

To cater for our ever-growing need for speed, car manufacturers are making vehicles that can go much faster – often up to 220km/h. This has coincided with a move to slower legal street speeds to counter the number of cars going too fast. We have introduced express trains for people who do not have time to stop at every station, and people now fly everywhere rather than do long drives through towns of 300 people, one garage and a cannon or statue in the park to remind us of the war.

11. Waking up

There is an old saying that the sleep requirement of the average human being is about five minutes more. There are varying views on how much sleep we actually need. Growing up we were all told eight hours, but many people claim to function quite proficiently on much less than that.

Typically, modern sleep deprivation issues are blamed on light bulb inventor Thomas Edison. Edison famously despised sleep and was quite chuffed that artificial light allowed him to cheat nature's night and day system. He reasoned that sleep was an acquired habit rather than a necessity. He is quoted as saying: "Cells don't sleep. Fish swim about in the water all night; they don't sleep. Even a horse doesn't sleep, he just stands still and rests. A man doesn't need any sleep." This view did not stop Edison falling asleep a fair bit in his workshop. There is a good chance he was completely wrong.

As humans deprive themselves of more and more sleep so they can fill their waking hours with more things, greater pressure is applied to alarm clocks to get us out of bed when we really don't feel like it.

Despite this, over the years alarm clocks have become indecisive and wishy-washy, worn down by decades of dealing with people at their worst moment of the day. Alarm clocks are regularly beaten, abused and hammered by their owners. Alarm rage afflicts about one in three people and there is no known cure.

As a kid I was given a traditional analogue wind-up alarm clock as a hand-me-down. It was very decisive. The alarm bell had apparently been stolen from outside a fire station. It was so loud that the sheer shock caused me to jump metres into the air. I'm sure neighbours on both sides ended up running into the backyard armed with garden hoses.

The alarm never went off when it was supposed to either, generally preferring the very early hours of the morning. Eventually, after a household revolt, it was banned and replaced with a digital version. Sometimes the old clanger still went off by itself. It was a beast that would not be silenced.

That old alarm clock was probably the last of a bold breed of morning wake-up devices that took no prisoners. This was an era when alarm clocks were held in great regard and were not to be messed with. You could pick them up and throw them across the room and they could keep coming back for more. "You will get up," it would be saying. "Do it now."

The digital alarm clock lacks this commanding attitude. For a start, it gives you a choice of either waking up to the radio or a buzzer. Most people choose the radio because the buzzer sounds like someone is using a grinder on your ear. But the alarm clock is no longer confident enough just to go off. Now there are options. Like the snooze button. This allows you to sleep-in just a few minutes more. Why people use the snooze button is not clear. If you have the choice of getting up later, why not just set the alarm for later?

On a recent trip, my room had an alarm clock with four snooze buttons, multiple reminder back-up alarms and choices of several different buzzer and radio options. The alarm unit resembled a small satellite and required a degree in aerospace engineering to operate. So I rang reception and asked for a human wake-up call instead. I didn't ask if they also did "snooze" calls five minutes later.

The human world is divided into two groups – morning people and everyone else. Everyone else is by far the biggest group. Morning people are a small and largely annoying minority who rise in the early hours of the morning and act fairly chirpy. They tend to make a lot of noise with pots and pans. Nobody is really sure what they do with the pots and pans, just that they are banging together at 4am in a fairly chirpy manner.

Everyone else spends their lives going to bed when they do not feel tired, and waking up when they do. Even though they have one every day, they dread mornings and resent having to get up. Most of this group secretly aspire to be morning people, and every New Year they vow to become morning people. This almost never happens.

12. Armless intentions

While the human body could generally be considered a triumph of engineering design, it has a couple of flaws that have managed to sneak through. That might be because man was created at the end of a long week after the Creator devoted his (or her) most creative and competent hours to tasks like light and water. By the time he/she got to man, the Creator would have been knackered and needing the seventh day to rest.

One of the most obvious design issues concerns the arm and what we are meant to do with it when we are sleeping.

Unless you sleep on your back (which apparently only a small percentage of the population do), the spare arm is just in the way. It presents a particular problem for the majority of the population who sleep on their sides. If you put it down beside you, your head lacks sufficient support and plops onto the pillow with undue gravity. You wake up feeling like you have hung upside down all night.

Alternatively, you put it under your head or pillow. But this brings serious risk that the arm will "fall asleep" through restricted blood flow, and hang lifeless in the morning as you push and prod it into action. It is possible that birds may be a more advanced species than humans. This is why they have learnt to sleep standing up rather than having to put a wing under the pillow.

13. Things people do

Once humans formed into a society and invented money, it became important for them to work to earn money for life's basics like eating and gambling. Many jobs serve a worthwhile purpose. Others seem to have been created purely to give people something to do. It is important for humans to have something to do. Otherwise they get bored and vandalise signs and railway carriages. In extreme cases, they phone talk-back radio.

To qualify as a job, a task generally has to be something that someone is prepared to pay you to do. In its most basic form, this begins with throwing newspapers, delivering leaflets, and singing Simon and Garfunkel songs on the street with a hat in front of you. Further up the work food chain is serving in fast-food restaurants, performing basic low-skilled tasks, and "running errands". These jobs are generally performed by young people who have not yet realised that these positions are no fun and pay very poorly.

The general rule of jobs is that the more you get paid, the less you are required to do. Very rich businesspeople can generally just swan around a lot and hire managers to do the actual work. Swanning involves some lunches and joining a club where you can be seen to be swanning. Often a large boat is involved (in the swanning, not the club).

While most people are employed by corporations and governments to perform a particular task, others are known as consultants and get paid to work for short periods to tell corporations and governments how they could be working better. This process generally involves the production of a thick report with charts recommending that further consultants be hired. These reports generally sit on a shelf until someone notices the same problem five years later and hires another group of consultants. This whole process serves no actual purpose but keeps quite a few people off the streets.

Tall People Don't Jump

People who cannot find a job are referred to as unemployed and receive a fortnightly cheque from the government. In less-enlightened times, these people were referred to as dole bludgers. This was a highly derogatory term that suggested these people are deliberately unemployed. This is generally not the case. Most humans actually want to work, because the first question asked in almost any encounter between previously unacquainted humans is: "What do you do?" If you have a job, it is easier to answer this question without lying.

Sometimes people are not rapt in their actual job titles and make up better titles to make them sound more impressive. Garbage men have become known as sanitation officers, tuckshop ladies call themselves nourishment consultants, dish washers are hygiene consultants, and road sweepers are highway environmental hygienists. Librarians have been known to be called competitive intelligence officers or knowledge coordinators.

Some jobs earn a lot of money because they have skills shared by only a few people. Surgeons fall into this category due to their ability to cut people open, fix them and sew them back together again. This should not be attempted at home. Lawyers are another group who enjoy high salaries because the things they do seem so complicated and convoluted that it is assumed the tasks are important and worth paying thousands of dollars for. The rules of any country or state are written in thousands of pages of legislation and only lawyers know where to find the obscure bits to get you off when you commit a crime. They are also highly trained in putting so many unnecessary words into a sentence that only other lawyers would have any chance of deciphering them. Modern society insists that everything is "official". Nobody really knows what it means, but it helps give humans a sense that everything is under control. This keeps thousands of lawyers employed continually creating and deciphering thousands of documents designed to fill up filing cabinets and make things "official".

One of the difficulties with putting people together in a workplace is that they may actually be less productive as a group than they are as individuals. This phenomenon is know as "social loafing" and is said to apply to everything from tug-o-war and workplaces to sporting teams. The theory goes that people reduce their output and motivation when they are part of a group because they assume they can pull a lesser weight. A researcher in the 1930s found that a person involved in a rope tug-o-war in a group of eight put in 50 per cent less effort than if he or she was pulling the rope alone. Another study of yelling found that a person shouting alone would make a 20 per cent greater effort than if he or she was one of six people shouting. Another found that someone sitting alone in a restaurant had a 20 per cent likelihood of leaving a tip, while the likelihood fell to 13 per cent when they were part of a group.

If you believe the social loafing theory, it probably follows that all workplaces should have a maximum of one person to achieve optimum productivity. Team sports should be abandoned in favour of tennis and badminton, and Solitaire should be the only game in town.

While the role of most jobs is fairly easy to grasp, in some cases it is not entirely clear what purpose the job serves. In these cases nobody ever asks the question, fearing they might be seen as idiots, or uneducated. For this reason, for many centuries orchestras have had conductors. Great conductors are acclaimed across the world as they stand at the front of the musicians waving their stick around. But non-music people are never sure exactly what they do, and are certainly too afraid to ask someone wielding a stick.

The musicians don't ever seem to look up. They have their music, they know when to play and what to play. What does that leave?

I thought perhaps the conductor was someone who could not play an instrument and kept hitting the triangle or tambourine at the wrong time. So they made him stand at the front and wave the stick around. It's the job you can't mess up.

The conductor also must go on the Kylie Minogue butt diet and work out, because during the whole performance the most dominant feature of the ensemble is the conductor's butt. Even the best orchestras can come unstuck if the conductor's butt is in poor shape. You just can't perform a great symphony with an inappropriate conductor's butt.

Of course, one of the best jobs in the world is being captain of your country's Davis Cup tennis team. Unlike other captains, you don't actually play. Your job is to sit in a chair and look worried. When one of your team loses a point, you stand up and look very worried. If things do not go your way, you complain. When your team wins a point, you jump up and down a few times and wave your arms about. When you win the tie, you drink lots of beer. Only former players are allowed to apply.

Then there are the security guards who sit outside businesses and events apparently armed only with a police-replica uniform and lunchbox. What do they do if there is trouble? Threaten the perpetrator with their lunchbox? While I'm sure they do a good job, not many of them look very threatening. They remind you of your uncle. Some look like they would turn placid if you fed them.

14. The beach

Humans have always been attracted to the beach. They like to look at it and live near it. They also like to sit in the ocean and let the waves break over them. Humans will do this for hours. They are not sure why, but everyone else is doing it too. Any property that has even fleeting glimpses of water is worth a lot more. In fact, all human civilisation pretty much starts at the water and works back from there.

The beach scene has changed a lot over the years. In decades past, thousands of people would just lie on the beach all day and burn themselves. This was known as sunbaking. Nobody is really sure why people did this. It seems to be a similar phenomenon to beaching whales. Humans would bake themselves en masse no matter how odd it seemed.

These days hardy anyone sunbakes. This is because sunbaking, like most things people used to enjoy, will probably kill you. Now you venture onto the beach only when it's already dark or if you have a structure resembling the Moscow Circus tent erected over your head. Alternatively, you don complete body armour, apply a factor 30+ sunblock designed to repel a nuclear attack, and wear sunglasses so dark you keep running into light poles.

Another of the big changes at the beach is the huge growth of boogie boards. When you hit the waves now, half of all the people in the water are boogie-boarding. The other half is diving all over the place trying not to get flattened by a boogie board. Children are generally very bad at driving boogie boards and will run into you regularly. Mostly they think this is very funny.

The boogie board is a bit like a stunted surfboard. It is great for people who like to see themselves as surfie types but are scared witless about actually standing up and hanging ten. With the boogie board, you at least have something under your arm as you run up and down the beach humming *Surf City* and trying to look like one of the local surfer lads. You can usually pick the non-genuine surfies by the tanless shirt lines on their arms and the unfaded board shorts with the price tag still hanging out the back.

People at the beach tend to develop strange rituals. Anyone over the age of about 15 does not arrive at the beach just in swimwear unless they have supermodel bodies, hail from Scandinavia or have no shame. Generally people hit the beach highly clad. They de-clad slowly until they get to the last bit of cover-up. The last thing always comes off at warp speed after a nervous look around to check no-one is watching. It is as if they expect the lifesaver to hold up a card giving them a score out of 10.

Today there seems to be a complete lack of consensus about what constitutes a suitable swimming costume. People, particularly men, will wear just about anything that will tolerate water exposure. This ranges from tiny budgie-smuggler swim togs to full body suits and giant shorts.

For some reason, most men over 50 tend to keep their swimming trunks for at least 30 years. In the 1960s, swimming shorts, like Holdens and washing machines, were obviously made to last. These "trunks" could be put in the drawer and brought out each summer for the annual holiday. They were solid and heavy and had a waist tie that could be loosened as each spare tyre was added.

Of course, a beach holiday would not be complete without fishing. I had managed to have "incomplete" holidays for 10 years, but my young children at the time finally convinced me to dust off the rod and reel and try again. The fish were apparently awake to this little caper. Someone had apparently told them why all the dead worms lined up at 3m intervals along the shore were shaped like hooks.

The thing that really spoils the beach is the sand. When you get within 50m of it, it jumps at you and infiltrates all aspects of your life. Your clothes start to feel sandy, your boots get full of it, and everything you eat is accompanied by that unmistakable sand-crunching sound.

Once your world has been infiltrated by sand, you can never really get rid of it. It stays in the bottom of bags, in the boot of your car, and sometimes in your hat. Sand also has a strange habit of getting into your sandwiches. This is apparently ironic.

15. Camping

Deep down, human beings harbour a desire to get back to nature. Mostly they are in love with a romantic notion of the Wild West, and sleeping under the stars while a cowboy plays songs about home while sitting around the campfire. In their minds, camping will put them at one with nature, answering the call of the wild and getting a chance to wear the designer "bush" clothes they picked up at an Anaconda sale.

There are two types of camping. The first is an authentic wilderness experience where you carry all your gear, lump around a genuine National Geographic compass and live off wild things that you kill with your bare hands. For most of us, this should be avoided. It would end up involving the emergency rescue helicopter, cliff-winching, and television footage that makes you look like Tom Hanks in *Castaway*.

The second is civilised camping. This is when you take all your wilderness gear and set it up in an advanced urban environment with manicured lawns, hot-water showers and a major supermarket and five-star restaurant no more than a block away. This gives us the illusion of roughing it, but without the snakes, spiders and painful rashes.

Civilised camping brings together three distinct groups who otherwise have nothing in common and generally should not be mixed together in confined space – retired folk, couples with young children, and teenagers with fifteen bucks and a Volkswagen.

The teenagers don't sleep because they are teenagers, the couples don't sleep because they have loud, restless children, and the retired folk don't sleep because everyone else is making so much noise. The end result is something like *The Osbornes* meets *Black Hawk Down*.

Camping grounds also bring out three different types of campers – the high level comfort seekers, the middle level rough-it-a-bit brigade, and the low-impact minimalists. The comfort seekers have five-star camping gear that skillfully recreates a palatial mansion, entirely in canvas. This group takes at least a full day and eight adults to erect the tent, which usually has four bedrooms (complete with king-size master bunks), a verandah, television room, gas-powered chandeliers and a double zip-up garage.

The middle level rough-it-brigade have a standard-issue Kmart tent with enough room to sleep and store a fold-up table, a light, an esky and a gas cooker. They nearly always have children and sometimes congregate in groups under a shared canvas common room where they talk and drink until the early hours in ever-increasing volumes.

The camping gear of the minimalists consists of a little tent with a tiny pile of gear outside. The little pile contains a loaf of bread, a saucepan, a bottle of alcohol and a box of matches. The inhabitants are usually male and they can be easily identified because their feet generally protrude out of the end of the tent and their wardrobe is a single pair of board shorts. They should be approached with caution any time before 11am.

Days at the camping ground are filled with countless hours and endless possibilities. In other words they are incredibly boring. In the urban wild of the camping ground, time is an abstract concept and campers have to develop special routines. To facilitate this, most camping grounds arrange for a guy in a ute to come at the same time every day to deliver ice. This keeps the campers focused and avoids a total breakdown of civilised society, a la *Lord of the Flies*.

The coming of the ice man is a very special and spiritual time. Most days, the campers don't need the ice but they buy it anyway. It is part of the camping experience and camaraderie. It is a time to mix with fellow campers and exchange stories about esky efficiency, beer temperature and the relative volume of mosquitoes the night before.

The ice can also provide hours of entertainment. When you run out of card games and have done more walking than Burke and Wills, you can just sit your ice on the ground and watch it melt. As a special treat, when the ice is fully melted you can sit and watch the grass grow where it sat.

During a rare recent camping trip I discovered another tactic to keep campers focused and involve them in shared activity – the push-button showers. These showers are designed to give campers the illusion of a warm shower without the actual benefits. Before you enter the shower you must push a button on the wall outside that corresponds with the shower cubicle you intend to enter. Then you must bolt into the shower and throw open the hot tap. The button is carefully calibrated to give you just enough time to get shampoo in your hair under warm water, but not enough to wash it off. As you are waiting for a spare shower, you hear a constant chorus of "d'oh" and "blast" (and various other French words) as the dream of a warm shower is shattered, cubicle by cubicle, camper by camper.

At this point you have the option of taking on the role of shower-button good Samaritan. This involves walking to the panel of buttons and pushing them, thus giving your fellow campers a second chance at the warm shower. The reaction is immediate, with the chorus of French obscenities replaced by "ahhhs" and "ohhhs" as the campers wallow in their improved circumstances.

16. The war against grass

Sometimes you have to wonder whether humans were really meant to be on this planet. In a sense they are totally out of place and seem to spend a lot of the time trying to wreck it, renovate it or generally fight its natural tendencies. It is possible the creation of the human race was just a big mistake that got out of control.

When you think about it, the early cavemen days of human civilisation were far more planet-friendly. Humans ate what they needed, burnt minimum fossil fuel and amused themselves with small-scale tribal wars and writing on the caves. Life was simple then. Sure, you starved sometimes and every so often got eaten by wild animals, but there was quality family time and children respected their elders.

Then everything changed. The Egyptians, Greeks and Romans had some critically-acclaimed civilisations and people started inventing wheels, toasters and aqueducts. Before long there were chains of takeaway outlets, philosophy, television, video games and the internet (not necessarily in that order). Rather than share the wild open plains, each human sought to own a tiny bit of it. On this tiny bit they put a square house surrounded by grass. Then for the rest of their lives they battled the grass.

As part of this battle, humans have decided it is a good idea to cover as much of the earth's surface as possible with concrete. This involves removing natural trees and greenery and replacing them with a hard grey surface that wears on your ankles and causes you to bleed if you fall over on it. It is not hard to see why this would happen. People would think: "Sure grass is nice to walk on and looks good, but the bloody stuff keeps growing and it contains bugs. We need to cover it with something that only earthquakes, nuclear weapons and large men with jackhammers can break."

Humans now have an insatiable desire for concrete. Concrete plants run all day and night all over the world supplying building sites, footpath construction trucks, slabs for houses, pillars for bridges and weighting for mob murder victims. Alas, it will still take many centuries to cover the earth's entire surface with concrete, so humans must still use a large amount of their discretionary time mowing the lawn.

There is something particularly brutal about mowing. In your yard there is a nice healthy chain of wildlife all happily eating each other, pollinating plants and making insect sounds. There are colourful birds singing in the trees, vast undulating plains of wondrous natural beauty and sunsets of crimson and gold. Then, there's me, in old shorts, holey straw hat and black thongs, pushing a noisy Victa which destroys everything in its path. I can't help feeling I don't quite fit in.

I think about lots of things while I'm mowing. I have to. When you live on a 3000sqm block of land, life is divided into two roughly equal parts – mowing and everything else. My only saving grace over recent years has been the drought, apparently caused by global warming, possibly linked to Al Gore's data projector running continually for five years. Our place got so dry even the artificial plants died.

Mowing has been a staple of mine since my early teens when I used to earn extra pocket money by setting the Victa loose on any yard that would have us. The big problem with spending so much time mowing is that mowers (like all mechanical equipment) were really never meant to work. Mowers will usually break down when your grass reaches a height of about 70cm. Then it's time for the tool box.

To be really honest, I don't know the first thing about fixing mowers, but every time the machine won't go I get out the tool box and undo every screw and bolt I can find. When I'm finished, I stand back and look at the disassembled collection of springs, nuts and washers thinking: "Hmmm, I wonder what all that stuff does." Then I put the whole thing in a plastic shopping bag and take it to the friendly man at the shop who turns it back into a mower. "What did you do?" he always asks. I shrug my shoulders and he nods knowingly. Mechanical clods like me have made him a very successful man.

How stupid is grass anyway? Every week I go along and cut it to pieces, and every week it shoots up again to get the same punishment. Grass just doesn't get it. Wouldn't you think that over the years it would just evolve and learn to not grow long? I'm sure the planet we were meant to be on was all Astroturf.

17. Not waving, ironing

In a moment of weakness many years ago, I volunteered to do the family ironing. This is not something I am proud of. Humans were never really meant to iron. Yet somehow we convinced ourselves that clothes must be flat and unrumpled. Once this happened, there was no turning back. The curse of the iron would be passed down through many generations. Few people would ever be truly happy again.

The introduction of the iron, like the cane toad, the rabbit and season four of *Lost,* was one of life's great mistakes. Before that, everyone must have just walked around in horribly crushed suits and dresses and thought nothing of it. Now if you walk around like that, people start putting money in your hat.

What was wrong with crushed clothes anyway? People were happier when they were crinkled. You couldn't tell the difference between a street derelict and a company executive. It was a classless society.

Of course, when you do the family ironing, you view the whole concept of clothes and the wearing thereof in a different light. In days BI (before ironing), I would think nothing of wearing a shirt once for an hour and throwing it in the wash. Not now. I wear them until they walk to the wash themselves or the council health inspectors come to the door and take them away. Sometimes the shirts get so bad I toss them in the wheelie bin, and the bin spits them out.

I'm kidding, of course. What really happens is you tend to buy clothes that either don't need ironing or you just iron the front and make sure your suit jacket stays on. The sad reality of ironing is you never finish it. If I iron four hours a week, I don't even reach the top of the basket. Occasionally, I do 20-hour ironing marathons and get about halfway down. There I usually find clothes the children grew out of two years ago (after they wore them once) and a collection of odd socks.

The odd socks in the ironing basket tend to explain why there are also so many odd socks in the folding basket. Every few months I am able to bring the two groups together for a tearful reunion. We take pictures, have cake and they exchange stories about being separated on the clothes line and their long, lonely wait for news of their partner. Some socks are never reunited. Their partners simply disappear. In this situation, "missing sock" posters are generally ineffective. In black and white, all socks look uncannily similar.

A common trait of ironing volunteers is you tend to have a hysterical reaction when anyone in the family wears ironed clothes. "How can you wear that?" you scream, "I've only just ironed it." This is because people who volunteer to do the ironing – at least those who have not yet been committed to the happy farm – have visions of a utopian world where things stay ironed.

Deep down we see ourselves as artists, and an ironed garment is like a completed masterpiece. In fact, I am thinking of approaching a local gallery to discuss a display of some of my more accomplished works. These could include a "best of" selection of *Lion King* T-shirts, assorted denim tops with tricky collars, and some fancy tablecloths that barely fit on the ironing board. Then, there's the biggie – the cotton dress with pleats. This would require the full glass-cabinet treatment and its own security guard. Print replicas would be sold in the gallery shop.

18. Cinemas

When you are a parent, one of the real pleasures in life is being able to escape to a movie that doesn't have any dwarfs, Dalmatians or puppets. The cinema that you took for granted pre-children suddenly becomes the ultimate getaway chamber where you can lose yourself into a digital world full of interesting people, occasional coarse language and adult themes.

The whole thing is set up like that. In some cinemas, even before the movie starts, that voice comes on and assures you that everything you possibly need is there. "You wanted a big screen," the voice booms, "You're looking at it." "You wanted Dolby sound. You're listening to it." "You wanted to pay $15 for a tiny ice cream. You just did." "You wanted noisy people to watch the movie with? They're sitting right behind you."
The biggest dilemma when you enter the cinema is choosing the right spot to sit. You are told from a very young age never to sit in the front row because you end up with a cricked neck and looking up the actors' noses. You can't sit in the back row because it's reserved for teenage boys trying to work out how they can get their arms around the girls sitting next to them. Most take at least the first hour trying to resolve whether they should use the lob and drop method or the forehand drive across the shoulder. Then they sit there stooped, uncomfortable and praying desperately that the Brut 33 they plastered under their arms goes the distance. You need to give these couples at least three rows of separation.

When you choose a seat, there is also the aisle dilemma. The aisle seats have advantages, but you spend most of the movie with your knees rubbing on your nose so the people sitting in the middle can get past you after they visit the candy bar. You get a better view from the middle of the row, but it is a difficult spot to sprint from as soon as the final credits start to roll. The final-credit sprint has long been a ritual for Australian moviegoers. Even when there are only 30 people in the cinema, the first hint of credits has the same impact as an Olympic starter's pistol. People think: "Holy cow, the credits – let's get out of here." Minties fly in all directions, slow people are trampled, and ushers with their tiny torches have to swing from the curtains to avoid a running-of-the-bulls-style fate.

Sometimes when you do this, you get caught by the false ending. About one in every 20 films has a false ending. These involve extra bits during the credits that are still part of the movie, but not really. There is no pre-warning that these are coming. It is like one of the concert encores that happen after some idiot has already turned on the house lights. The false ending is sometimes out-takes. Other times it is snapshots of what became of the characters in the film. The strangest false ending of all is when the cast assembles to sing a song that is totally out of context with the movie. When this happens, you just continue your stampede from the cinema. Nothing good ever came from a closing credit all-cast song.

The people who sell the movie tickets always seem pleasant but, despite more than 20 years of trying, I have never been able to strike up a conversation with any of them. Say something like "two adults please" and they are okay. But try something more intellectual like "How about that game last night?" and they stare right through you and start to twitch. And when you walk up to the ticket box, they always ask the same question: "Yes?" What sort of a question is that? I must admit though, as a former journalist, I was always tempted to use it as an opening question for an interview. Maybe I should have shouldered up to the Prime Minister, stuck the tape recorder under his or her nose and just said: "Yes?" And if that didn't work, "How about that game last night" might have been a useful fallback.

19. Clapping

As humans evolved and started entertaining each other, it became necessary to develop ways to acknowledge appreciation of this entertainment. This resulted in the invention of clapping. Historians, anthropologists and physical therapists have differing views on the origins of clapping. There is also disagreement on whether it is an inherent human behaviour or learnt by babies through observation.

One theory is that clapping evolved from primates stamping and slapping their bodies when they were in a state of excitement. It is also often attributed as the first means by which humans made any type of music. This is because the early cavemen were generally poor and could not afford pianos. They did, however, mostly have hands.

As early as the third century BC there are references to plaudite, which translates to applause, and the Romans almost certainly clapped when someone in the arena was skewered or eaten by a lion.

Even though hand-clapping is a fairly basic form of noise creation, there are a number of subtle variations. Children learn to "fairy clap" with two fingers. This is because teachers are generally stressed and burnt out, and the noise associated with 40 clapping pre-teens would freak them out.

There is also "polite applause", which is a low impact form of clapping generally reserved for poor performances and bad jokes. This contrasts with genuine applause, which involves heavy hand contact and generally acknowledges performances that are genuinely entertaining, or comes in response to a sign held up in front of a studio audience.

Popular music artists have an obsession with clapping and will generally spend a large proportion of their concerts trying to get the audience to clap along with the song. The audience hates this because they have paid $150 to hear someone sing and all they can hear is a whole lot of clapping. To make matters worse, only about one third of the audience can clap in time, so this very quickly descends into an uncoordinated nightmare clapfest. The whole thing usually peters out half way into the song, except for two people who are concentrating so hard at keeping the beat that they don't notice they are the only ones still going. At the end of the show, these people can remember nothing of the concert but are fairly sure they clapped in time.

20. Opening a jar

Humans tend to keep a lot of things in jars. Mostly this is a good thing. Jars keep things sealed and dry and can be easily stored in fridges and cupboards. They are airtight, and some foods last many years inside them.

The jar strategy can, however, come unstuck when you have to remove the actual lid. Almost since the invention of jars, the removing of the jar lid has been an important test of male strength. Women mostly cannot remove jar lids and have to call on a man to do it. The man is then required to do a very male swagger and rip the lid off as if it requires no exertion whatsoever.

Naturally, as with most behaviour designed to protect the male ego, things do not always go that well. Sometimes the jar is just too tight and even the brute strength of a male cannot budge it. This is really embarrassing. In this situation, most men will not give up. They will keep working at the lid until their fingers are worn through to the bone and their tendons are a tangled mess. They will put boiling water on the lid, find giant spanners in the shed to twist it off, and use all manner of cloth to get a better grip. If all else fails, they will "accidentally" drop the jar on the floor and break it. This is usually associated with a contrived swearing outburst. Once the jar is broken, there is no further need to remove the lid.

If a male cannot remove a jar lid first go, there is an established protocol of excuses he must work through to try to save face. The most popular is greasy hands. It is a well-established scientific fact that nobody can open a jar with greasy hands. It is equally well established that hardly anybody ever has greasy hands (although fewer people know this). It is not generally necessary to explain the source of the greasy hands. Once you have established that your hands are greasy, it is fairly easy to make a tactical withdrawal. Onlookers will think: "He can't possibly open the jar, he has greasy hands."

The worst possible outcome in a tight jar situation is when the male is the first to attempt the jar and cannot do it. Often, at this point, a female will offer to try. Men tend to resist this and say things like: "Well if I can't do it, I can't see much sense in you trying." This reaction causes the female to erupt internally into feminist, bra-burning, men-hating stupor that concentrates the body's adrenalin and gives her the strength of 50 monkeys. In this state she rips off the jar lid with ease, taking equality forward 10 years and putting the male ego back 50. Men can never accept the reality of this situation and will retort: "I must have loosened it." No one has yet mastered saying this line without sounding lame. There is, of course, no such thing as a loosened lid.

21. Wet paint

The most useless sign in the human inventory is the "wet paint" sign. This sign is used universally to indicate actual wet paint. Despite this, when confronted with this sign, humans will almost always put their hand on the paint just to check. It is nearly always wet. This seems to come as a surprise. The brain seldom stores this information for future reference. It will encourage you to touch the next one as well.

22. Tying knots

Comedian Jack Benny described a Boy Scout troop as 12 little kids dressed like schmucks following a big schmuck dressed like a kid. This was perhaps a little harsh given the number of dedicated volunteers who have given their time.to the scouts. There was a time when joining a scout troop was a mainstream aspiration for boys around the world. The movement still exists, but fewer young people are prepared to dress in uniform, don woggles and stand in a circle doing chants.

The movement always struggles to get new leaders. This is mainly because the leaders must wear khaki shorts with a belt. It is very hard for grown men to look good in khaki shorts with belts, particularly if they have knobbly knees. In the bush, the scout leader must command respect and authority. It is very difficult, however, to command respect and authority when people are laughing at your knees.

The main purpose of the scouts appears to be earning merit badges and learning to tie knots. Pretty much anyone who has been in the scouts can tie a reef knot, a sheaf bend, a clove hitch and a bowline. Approximately none of them has ever been called on to tie these knots in any practical real-world situation, but they feel superior knowing they could tie them if called on in an emergency.

Merit badges are awarded to scouts who perform a series of tasks and challenges. The main purpose of the merit badge is to make the shoulder of the uniform more colourful and to laud it over other scouts with fewer merit badges.

Scouts must also learn bush survival skills. This involves putting up a tent and learning to live off the land eating only chocolate bars and cans of food purchased from Woolworths. Scouts also must hike and learn about nature, bush toilets and stinging nettles (the latter preferably not at the same time as they are learning about bush toilets).

23. Umbrella protocol

When it is raining, the average area occupied by a human being increases by about 600 per cent as they raise umbrellas to keep the rain off their heads. Humans enjoy having water on their heads when they are showering or swimming. But when they are walking down the street, they will avoid water at any cost.

Once the umbrellas are up, there is no longer enough room in the average city street to fit all the humans who wish to traverse it. This requires activation of city umbrella protocol. Umbrella protocol dictates that you must move your umbrella up and down to avoid clashing with the umbrellas approaching you. Sometimes this gets out of sync and the umbrellas clash, becoming entangled and uncomfortable. People get very annoyed when this happens and swear under their breath.

The umbrella clash can be avoided by wearing a raincoat, but most humans would rather soak than don one of these. It is very hard to look cool in a raincoat. You tend to look like an out-of-place jackaroo, or a slightly freakish version of Little Red Riding Hood.

No matter how much you practise, no brain seems capable of storing umbrella protocol data. This appears to be a fault of evolution. The human body has no natural feature to repel rain, and apparently rejects any artificial attempt to do so.

Modern umbrellas have become highly compact and foldable so they can be stored in a drawer or a handbag. Humans tend to have a lot of umbrellas because they inevitably leave them at home in a drawer and have to buy another one when it actually rains. Thankfully, they fold very small and you can store a lot of them in a drawer.

Before folding umbrellas we had large and sturdy varieties that could withstand most squall conditions. Folding umbrellas are wiry and bendy and do not do well in wind. A strong gust can flip them upwards like a frightened starfish, rendering them totally useless to repel rain. In this situation, people will maniacally battle the umbrella to pull it back into shape. By then they are soaked to the skin.

Despite the relative frequency of rain, most human clothing has no tolerance for water. In fact, the more expensive the outfit, the less is the inbuilt rain tolerance. Faced with rain, suits crinkle, leather and suede come out in a rash, dresses run, and T-shirts become see-through. Despite many centuries of rain, humans never seem to actually expect it. "Hang on," they think. "Water is falling from the sky. That doesn't sound right. Someone should fix that."

24. The spirit of Christmassy

Most of our perceptions of Christmas come from childhood when the summer season is full of magic, colour, carols, Santa Claus and presents. As we get older and wiser, the magic gets harder to recapture each year, despite our best efforts. As a result, humans are constantly complaining that they don't feel "Christmassy" yet.

Christmassy, a word that doesn't seem to have made the dictionary, describes the state of mind, emotion and joy that we expect to feel as of right during December. To achieve this, we get into a ritual of Christmassy things. We buy lots of presents, attend every Christmas carols night we can find, play the Bing Crosby *White Christmas* tape until it creaks and squeaks, and cover our houses with hundreds of coloured lights.

But often it doesn't work. "I'm still not feeling Christmassy," someone will complain.

So you bring out the big guns – *Home Alone* (the original), *Miracle on 34th Street* and *Jingle All the Way*. You read *T'was the Night Before Christmas* multiple times, you volunteer at a soup kitchen, and put a present for poor people under a tree at the department store. If Christmassy still hasn't kicked in by Christmas Eve, you play your last card – watching the Carols by Candlelight on television.

Then before we know it, Christmas Day arrives. There are gifts everywhere, lots of food to eat, children trying to play with everything at once, and the rounds of relatives. The next day, as we start the Christmas wind-down, we start to miss the wondrous weeks of December and we think what a great Christmas it was.

I have to admit to being a fairly substantial Christmas fan. I love the whole bit – decorating the tree, buying the ham, eating too much and going shopping at midnight, just because you can. To be perfectly honest though, Christmas in Australia is a time of really weird cultural rituals. We sit around singing about white Christmases, when the closest we ever get to anything white is that stuff you spray on your windows and spend the next 12 months scraping off with a razor blade. It's also the time of year when people are most likely to kill or mug each other – usually because they don't like their presents or, more likely, they don't like their relatives.

Then there's the Christmas shopping. For some reason we worry every Christmas that we haven't bought enough. Will the relatives think we are giving them too cheap a present? Will our Christmas lunch be compared unfavourably with what the cousins did last year? Will anyone notice that the chips and lollies are generic brand?

During December shopping, all the usual rules of human courtesy go out the window. People are generally quite happy to barrel aside old ladies or hog disabled car parks if they believe it will get them the perfect turkey or the last Christmas cake.

The biggest fear at Christmas is getting a present from someone unexpectedly (i.e. when you don't also have one for them). You should just accept this with grace and gratitude. Instead, most people just stare at it for a while as their mind decides whether to just say thank-you, own up that they didn't get anything, or make up a lame story about their present being in the mail. In these circumstances, nobody ever believes their present is in the mail. This is because it pretty much never is.

To overcome the unexpected present dilemma, some people keep ready supplies of generic, gender-neutral presents that can be produced at very short notice and allow you to emerge from the whole situation with some self-respect. Generic presents usually consist of chocolates, nuts, tiny biscuits from Europe, and mini jars of jam made from obscure fruit varieties. Nobody ever believes the generic present was actually meant for them. But they generally accept it with good grace and store it for the following Christmas when it can be re-gifted as their own generic present.

By December 24, most people are so desperate to complete their Christmas purchases they will buy just about anything draped in tinsel and flashing lights. After Christmas, they buy more of the same stuff for 70 per cent less.

Each year, people also vow not to buy their fathers socks and hankies. Socks and hankies have become so clichéd for fathers that nobody is game to choose them as gifts any more. Instead, they search the shops for days looking for something else and end up with talking ashtrays, one of those things you shake to make it snow, or a CD of someone who looks old enough for your father to know, and possibly like. He receives the gift with quiet gratitude, throws it into the top of his cupboard, and then spends the year wearing a holey pair of socks and blowing his nose on his shirt. This is because males have been genetically programmed to receive socks and hankies as gifts. They are not capable of buying these items themselves and don't even know where to look. The Christmas underwear revival is an equally vital ingredient of any father's yearly clothes plan. Without it, there are long, hard months of hitching and adjusting as last year's stock battles chronic elastic-fatigue syndrome. If this gets really bad, the father will eventually relent and buy some underwear. This is a task he always finds embarrassing. It messes with the whole underwear mystery.

The most hazardous place at Christmas is undoubtedly the department store perfume section. It is always heavily guarded by aggressive, pleasant-smelling sales people wielding perfume bottles the size of bazookas. They are trained not to let you out of there without a case of Chanel No 5. Unfortunately, I have a pretty bad sense of smell, and all perfumes seem to smell like a car deodoriser. It wouldn't surprise me if the whole lot is made in one big bucket and they just scoop it into containers with different names. As a result, I always choose perfume based on what the bottle looks like. This seldom ends well.

Of course it would not be Christmas without Christmas carols and a story about some childcare centre banning the carols in case they offend minority groups. I have never been really sure why Christmas would offend minority groups. What is not to like about Frosty the Snowman? Or should that be Frosty the Snowperson now? Perhaps it is the potential double entendres in the names. Silent Night, for example, might be grossly insulting to the hearing-impaired. White Christmas could be considered a racially-charged affront to indigenous people. Deck the Halls with Boughs of Holly might be mistaken for a violent and sordid tale about a barbaric attack on the Hall family using tree branches. The Herald Angels might be mistaken for bikies.

The other truly Australian Christmas tradition is the hot-baked

Christmas dinner. It is 40 degrees in the shade and Australians have their ovens on full-blast in the interests of keeping up European traditions. Christmas may indeed be a bad time of year for turkeys, but each year, somehow, the spirit of Christmassy finds us. So do people from Indian call centres.

Obsessions

25. Stuff

The biggest enemy of the modern household is stuff. Stuff breeds like a noxious weed, and left unchecked will quickly cover every flat surface in the home. When you take away all the trimmings in life, it really comes down to a battle between you and the stuff. Usually you lose.

Stuff can come in many forms: catalogues, newspapers, magazines, books, brochures, knick-knacks, leftovers from broken appliances, stray clothing, tapes, videos, recycling that you really should take out, vouchers for free food at places you never intend to eat, receipts, lotto forms ... and on it goes.

I suspect that if the average Australian adult sat in the same spot for more than six hours, he or she would completely disappear under stuff. It also is the reason the average Australian family moves every five years. This is the only way it can keep one step ahead of the stuff. The move allows the family to take trailer load after trailer load of acquired stuff to the dump or the charity bin. It also allows them to change address and keep the new one from all the junk mail companies for at least a few weeks.

Of course, if you have children, the battle against stuff becomes unwinnable no matter how many times you move. Kids are like stuff fertiliser. When you have them, the only way to keep your house clean is to hire someone to follow each child around with a broom, vacuum cleaner and wet rag.

Toddlers are the worst. The average 18-month-old can totally destroy a house in less than four minutes. Toddler stuff is in a category all of its own. Sometimes it is hoarded in secret locations which lull you into a false sense that it has disappeared. But hours later the soggy biscuit re-emerges from nowhere and is left in wait like a slimy parent trap which the father will inevitably put his foot in. When you first have a toddler, you quickly realise there is a key difference between the outlook of the small child and the adult. Adults generally regard neat as the normal state of being, while toddlers are bent on restoring everything to its natural state of chaos.

Of course, sometimes you need just a temporary break from the household stuff and this is why every 12 months or so you hire a unit at the beach. The trouble is, when you go to close the car boot, you realise all the stuff has come with you. Even worse, when you go to leave the beach a week later there is even more of it. This is particularly the case if the children pack their own bags.

Parent: "Do you have your toothbrush, underwear, clothes, towel and sunscreen?"
Child: "No, I forgot about those."
Parent: "So what's in the bag?"
Child: "Just stuff."

Of course, what else? To overcome the stuff affliction, humans have invented storage space. Most people will not purchase a house unless it has lots of storage space. Storage space is used to hide stuff. If you have storage space, particularly secret cupboards and boxes, you can take all the stuff off the benches and put it in the storage space. This doesn't quite get the stuff out of your life, but it at least hides it and gives you the impression that your life is free of stuff clutter.

The amount of stuff people have is in direct proportion to the amount of storage space available. The only thing humans hate more than stuff is empty cupboard space. If you have empty cupboard space, you feel compelled to go out and buy more stuff. This allows you to complain to everyone that you never have enough storage space.

26. Collecting

Many humans take acquiring stuff so seriously that it becomes an affliction known as collecting. Collecting is like other hoarding, except the person acquires a lot of similar things. This can be everything from old machinery and coins to toys, pop culture memorabilia and buttons.

The greatest collecting scam is stamp collecting. Most kids at some stage in their childhood start collecting stamps. This is generally because someone has told them if they collect stamps "someday" they might be worth something".

For a while you believe this. There are large, colourful stamps from Poland (or Polska as the stamp says), there are ones from America with the Statue of Liberty, and Australian stamps with kangaroos that date back to before your grandparents were born. These must be worth something one day.

But alas, every other child in the country has the same stamps. Even after you have had your stamps for 15 years, you can still find the same 50-year-old stamps in packs of 300 at a department store for $1.50. You can go to the flea market and buy them for five cents, and you can get them at every garage sale as soon as every other kid who thought their stamps would be worth something "someday" gives up and tries to get something back on their $15 stamp album investment.

Stamp authorities also release stamps in special collector packs with multiple stamps, or placed on an envelope and called a "first day cover". These are only envelopes. There are no covers. It is unclear why they are called first day covers, or why in fact anyone collects them.

Collecting coins is not much better. You find a penny that went out of circulation in 1966 and you think you can retire in a beachside condo. That is until you get to the markets and see a guy selling the same pennies in giant buckets for 10 cents each.

Collecting was once about finding things that already existed. Now things are made just for collecting. For any well-selling musical CD or DVD movie there is inevitably a "Collector's Edition". This edition is no different than the other editions except it has different packaging. This relies on obsessed collectors wanting every version of something they collect. As soon as there is a collector's edition, they must have it.

Adults who collect toys generally do this because they still like to play with toys and don't want to be locked up or socially ostracised. This is a Catch 22 for these collectors because toys apparently lose their collector value as soon as someone plays with them. The only good toy is a mint toy. If you keep it in the box, it might be worth something one day.

27. Because they are there

Once speed limits were introduced on roads, many humans felt unnecessarily restrained. "Sure we know every K over is a killer," they thought, "But what if there was a way I could go faster without killing anyone?" Such thinking resulted in the invention of theme park rides.

Theme park rides generally involve locking humans in some sort of metal cage and throwing them all over the place for several minutes. During the ordeal, many humans scream and ask to be let out. Sometimes vomiting follows. When the experience is finished, the humans line up at a different ride to repeat the sensation.

If aliens arrived on earth and visited theme parks, they would logically conclude that these places were some form of torture facility, reserved for the worst criminals. They would be totally baffled to discover that humans actually paid to be locked in a cage and thrown around.

There are varying theories on why humans are attracted to theme parks. One of these is: "Because they are there." In fact, "Because they are there" has long been used to explain many human pursuits. For centuries, humans have climbed mountains because they are there. They have also crossed deserts and icy wastelands for similar reasons. Sometimes they use it as an excuse to eat dessert.

When it comes to theme park rides, not only do people feel the need to torture themselves, but fairly obsessively want others to join the torture. If people are reluctant, they are usually called chickens. It is unclear why reluctant theme park ride participants are called chickens. It is possible that chickens also do not like to partake in theme park rides. This seems a fairly logical thing, even though chickens have a much smaller brain. The whole thing tends to prove that a large, sophisticated brain does not necessarily result in sounder decisions.

No theme park would be complete without fatty food and sugar drinks. This seems quite logical in the circumstances. If you are going to punish your body on the outside, why not give the inside a whacking as well. That will teach it.

At this point you must begin to ask what the brain is up to while all this is going on. During the theme park ride, the brain is like the deck of the Starship Enterprise during one of those Star Trek alien attacks. You can almost hear Scotty saying (please imagine a thick Scottish accent here): "Captain, she's takin' a terrible beatin'. I don't think she'll hold. We don't have the power. She canna take much mooore."

At the end of the ride, Captain Kirk would say: "Damage report?" and Scotty would say: "It's a wee miracle captain; we don't seem to have any damage. But don't do that again sir because I fear she won't hold together." At this point, Mr Spock would have something to say about the logic of getting into a cage and being thrown around for no apparent purpose. The

Tall People Don't Jump

Lost in Space robot would say that it does not compute. The chickens would justifiably act superior.

Over time, theme park rides have become faster and higher to meet the growing human demand for nausea and screaming. In the early days, the rides were confined to merry-go-rounds. These were mechanical rides that just went in circles while the participants rode mechanical horses. Sometimes the horses also went up and down. At the time, this was considered extreme.

After a while, humans got bored with merry-go-rounds. "Sure the merry-go-round goes round in circles and plays annoying music," they reasoned, "but is there a way to make the ride more exciting?"

Eventually someone came up with the idea of turning the merry-go-round on its side and letting the seats dangle down. This became known as the Ferris wheel. The Ferris wheel adds to the thrills because it has height, but when it is full it can take a long time to get people on and off so you spend a lot of time dangling. Sadly, little good ever came from dangling.

Next came the roller coaster. This involved putting cars and little trains onto high tracks and using gravity to shoot them around the tracks very fast. For a while this was the ultimate thrill ride. Eventually, however, it lost its novelty value because urban taxi drivers adopted a similar approach to daily transport. In the modern era, teenagers will generally only go on theme park rides that have the g-force of a space shuttle take-off and turn their inner ear into a milkshake.

For some humans, even the theme park ride is not enough of a thrill. Many need to put themselves at actual risk with extreme sports, and jumping out of airplanes. These daredevils often justify their risky behaviour on the basis that to feel alive, they must risk actual death.

People used to train for weeks so they could jump out of an airplane on their own. Now the sport has introduced tandem jumping, which involves a novice being strapped to someone who actually knows what they are doing and jumping together. This sounds rather disconcerting. When you are plummeting towards the ground with the full force of gravity, being strapped to someone who might fall on top of you sounds like a bigger risk than just throwing on the parachute, pulling the rip cord and taking your chances with the big empty sky.

28. Planet pandemonium

Humans have always been fascinated by space. This is partly because the space industry has a knack of whipping the population into a frenzy over galactic events that sound pretty exciting. I think this is largely because astronomers don't get out much and spend a lot of time in dark rooms staring into space.

In 1986 we were rallied to look into the skies ready for Halley's Comet which was coming by for the first time in 76 years. We had in mind trails of light across the sky, deeply spiritual reminders of our insignificance in the broader cosmos and exciting tales for future grandchildren. Instead we got a blob. Through a really strong telescope we got a bigger blob with a small tail. It wasn't even a particularly spiritual blob. And it made us feel superior to the universe. A comet like that we could put out with a garden hose.

Then there was the meteor shower a few years ago. We all got up at 2am for the promised "nature's own fireworks". But all we saw were two tiny streaks of light spread over an hour as the family huddled in the backyard. Duped again. Late in 2008 we were urged to look skyward because two planets and the crescent moon were just in the right place to form a smiley face. This one turned out to be true. Perhaps this was a message from the universe for us all to be happy.

Then we were whipped into a frenzy over Mars being closer than it had been in 60,000 years. Of course this meant it was "only" 55,760,220km away. For astronomers this was really exciting. Everyone else just went back to bed.

In fact, I have come to realise over time that all exciting astronomical discoveries are blobs. These are either tiny blobs in the sky, blurred photographs of blobs taken by the Hubble telescope or artists impressions of blobs. Every few days the space industry discovers a new blob. Some years ago they announced that the reason there are so few small galaxies in the universe was that they kept getting eaten by big galaxies. This came complete with an artist's impression of a large galaxy blob swallowing a small galaxy blob for anyone unfamiliar with the concept of eating. It was never really clear if this was a good or a bad thing. There is, however, something vaguely unnerving about being eaten by a galaxy.

Thankfully, in space years, pretty much anything that you discover either won't have an impact for millions of years or already happened several million light years ago and it just took a while for the evidence to reach us. There is also every chance that anything we learn about the universe will be disproved a few years later. Every few years, for example, someone announces that the universe is several billion years older or younger than first thought. This is announced with significant fanfare and earnestness. But what are supposed to do? Sorry Mr Universe, no more birthday cake for you?

Then there was the announcement that Australian astronomers had come up with the most accurate calculation ever of the number of stars in the universe. There are 70 thousand million million million of them. My first reaction was: "That sure is a lot of stars". In fact people around the world would have been shaking their head in wonder and saying "Yep, it's a lot of stars all right, a bloody lot of stars".

My personal favorite was the announcement that scientists had discovered a large area of space that contained absolutely nothing. The discovery caused considerable excitement in the space community. The University of Minnesota said the big black hole was nearly a billion light years across, making it quite a large expanse of nothing. Comedian Jerry Seinfeld may well decide to make a sitcom about it.

The space industry generally consists of several thousand scientists and several thousand public relations practitioners whose job it is to establish the importance of each space discovery in a bid to attract more money from governments and rich people. Often the discovery is said to just add to the sum of mankind's knowledge. Most people like the idea of having a large sum of knowledge. They may not ever personally have this knowledge but when they walk into a library they are comforted that there are quite a lot of books, suggesting quite a few people know quite a few things that might come in handy one day.

If the space discovery is particularly marginal they will generally find a way to relate it to medical research or experiments being conducted by American school children. If that fails they bring out the big guns, warning that one day the earth will die and we need to find other planets where we can live. They also warn that the earth could get hit with an asteroid and it is important we keep looking into space in search of these asteroids. If we find them in time we could fire nuclear weapons at them. Based on research involving movies, this most likely will not work. We would be better off sending a motley oil drilling crew to land on the asteroid and blow it up from the middle. If they were successful they would never have to pay tax again. In fact, if they were unsuccessful there wouldn't be a whole lot of reason to pay tax either.

The survival fear is fed by announcements every few years that an asteroid has been found that will probably nearly miss the earth in 40 years time. A near miss, in space terms, is hundreds of thousands of kilometres away. Again it is never really clear what we are supposed to do with this information. We could panic for 40 years but the stress would probably kill us before the asteroid.

Finding another planet is equally fraught. For a long time we put our hopes on Mars. Mars is close enough to fly to and looks fairly friendly in the sky. Unfortunately, when a space machine finally landed on it, it was pretty much all desert. Since then there have been suggestions that the planet contains water and some life. Unfortunately the life is, at best, bacteria and microscopic creatures. This is very disappointing. We always had our heart set on little green men.

Thankfully scientists with very large telescopes have found a couple of planets on the other side of the universe that may have similar characteristics to earth. Such news always comes as a huge relief. Unfortunately, when you read the fine print, these planets are usually millions of kilometres away and would take several hundred years to reach in a rocket. This means if we sent families there to repopulate, there would be several generations of children asking "are we there yet?" before any resettlement could be done.

The other possibility is that aliens will find us before we have to find them. This is based on the view that they might have better technology and faster space ships. Alternatively they might just be able to beam around space like Star Trek. To help contact these aliens, Earth has shot the Beatles song *Across the Universe* out into space. This is quite ironic. Aliens, however, might miss the subtlety and just blow us into a million pieces to stop the bloody racket.

While officially we like the idea of finding some aliens and having a white tie White House dinner with them, the lesson from science fiction is that this seldom ends well. In fact, as a human culture, we have never had high hopes for aliens. In popular culture aliens are pretty much always ugly. These ugly aliens are almost always bad and hostile. Even when aliens look attractive you know they are using some sort of very advanced alien technology to appear that way. Underneath they are like large lizards that nearly always eat humans or are obsessed with anal probes. And when they pretend to be friendly we know that is because they are softening us up for an invasion, to steel all of our minerals or to collect further anuses for probing.

Alien enemies can also be robots. The Daleks of Dr Who were probably the high point of television aliens. The low point was the Green Lady on Lost in Space who seemed to have had a nasty accident with a Frisbee. The annoying Jar Jar Binks from Star Wars is a close second. While NASA spends billions looking for aliens, deep down we only want to find aliens that are human. If we find ugly or robot aliens we will probably not invite them to come over. Presidents would inevitably avoid photo shoots with aliens who look like lizards. No votes in that.

Much of space research seems to revolve around seeking a greater understanding of the origin of the universe. The universe is a really difficult thing for people to understand. We know it is bigger than we could possibly imagine and full of stuff. But is there anything outside of the universe? What was there before the universe? How can anything just go on forever? And why are we on this strange blue planet in the middle of nowhere surrounded by darkness, a few planets and a giant sun that keeps us alive and burns us in the summer?

A popular explanation for the birth of the universe is the big bang theory. This revolves around a belief that making something as large as the universe would have made a fair bit of noise.

Most space people talk with great fondness about the 1960s when mankind first landed on the moon. This was the peak of public interest. American beat the Russians, kept to the timetable and declared that stepping onto the moon's surface was one small step for man and also one giant leap for him. Ever since, the space industry has struggled to get the same sort of attention. It keeps sending shuttles into space, mainly to test the impact of weightlessness on a series of high school science experiments, but this is generally no fun. It still seeks to come up with deep and profound reasons to spend billions of dollars sending off rockets and taking pictures but these sound increasingly unconvincing. Every few years it talks about going back to the moon but this would take more than a decade to achieve, apparently because somebody lost the map and the video footage.

United States presidents have traditionally liked talking about space because it diverts attention from the earth and its economy. Most new presidents announce at some stage in their term that they hope to put a man on Mars. The timeframe for this is always after their terms finishes. This clears the way for the next president to make the same declaration with no need to ever actually achieve the target.

In the meantime, the NASA continues to send probes into deep space to send back pictures. In one frenzy of activity, it managed to put two vehicles on Mars in the space of a few days, potentially creating the planet's first traffic jam. The Mars probes arrive on the planet in a giant jumping castle clad in bubble wrap that bounces around the planet like a super ball. Once it comes to rest, a toy car emerges and starts searching for life. This is apparent done with a giant robotic megaphone that screams: "Is anybody here?" The current vehicles have lasted longer than expected but generally these toy cars last only a few days before their batteries go flat. Future missions may have to be manned by Duracell or Energizer rabbits with drums in an attempt to achieve longer battery life.

29. Waiting for the windfall

Most humans spend a significant part of their lives hoping for a windfall. A windfall is a sudden rush of significant cash that allows you to buy all the things you always wanted to impress the neighbours.

The most sought-after windfall is the Lotto win. Each week millions of people put in their Lotto numbers in the hope that they can defy the one-in-a-billion odds and all their numbers come up. Of course most people never win but they are very excited by the possibility and watch the numbers fall every week in the genuine belief that they might win.

Others gamble on the stock market, hoping that the company they are investing in will suddenly be worth lots more and they can buy a yacht and start holidaying in cities with French-sounding names.

The stock market is a series of large electronic boards with numbers surrounded by stressed middle-aged men in suits who mostly have ulcers. Stock prices go up and down depending on whether most of the middle-aged men in suits are yelling "sell" or "buy". There never seems to be enough room at the stock market so people are crammed together like cattle and the noise is so bad they have to scream into the phones. The noise is so bad because everyone is screaming into the phones. If everyone talked normally and sat down the stock market would seem more like a public library but this would be less fun to watch.

Most of the time people around the board talk up the value of the market even if they don't believe it. This is known as a "bull" or bulldust market. When this happens people are happy because the "paper value" of the stocks that they own is worth more, making them feel superior because everyone likes more valuable paper.

The bulldust market continues until someone, anyone, spreads a rumour that the market is about to collapse. At this point everybody sells, causing the market to collapse. A bad market is known as a "bear" market because bears are very bad and sometimes they eat you.

Once the market turns into a bear, the men in suits look at it and say: "Boy those stocks look cheap. Let's buy them while they are cheap – BUY!" These types of buying and selling frenzies, which have little to do with the actual real world, are used to determine the state of the world economy. Politicians are always reluctant to comment on the market because they are perceived to have inside information and their comments might be misinterpreted. If the President, for example, looks worried when he is talking about the market, the men in suits go into a frenzy. "The President looks worried," they think. "Something must be very bad – SELL". When the President is in a good mood they think that he must know something good about the stock market. "The President seems very happy," they think. "That can only mean one thing – BUY!"

When the market is in a frenzy it can lose thousands of points in a week. Nobody knows what a point is but it is generally accepted that they are not good to lose. It is also bad if the All Ordinaries and Wall Street are down. When these are feeling really down it causes Depression.

Big investors are considered fair game in the stock market but when the market drop impacts on "mum and dad investors" a market slump is considered a major problem. Mum and dad investors are ordinary Australians whose only interest in the stock market is the $400 worth of shares they own in Telstra. When these shares fall in value it is considered a national crisis and hundreds call radio talkback to blame the government.

Sometimes a subprime lending market is created when banks in America give thousands of dollars to poor people who can't pay it back. When this happens they act surprised and struggle to explain why. The Americans then pass the losses around the world because they can. The whole thing is generally recorded in a Mike Moore documentary.

30. Free

Humans spend most of their lives trying to get into the positive side of an imaginary ledger. Sometimes people will ask them: Are you winning today? This basically is asking: "Are you on the right side of the ledger today?" In their minds humans are constantly adding up the ledger. If something goes wrong in their day that sits on the downside of the ledger. When something goes right, it is the upside. Most of their lives are spent trying to stay on the upside.

For most people, the most failsafe way to stay on the upside is to get something really cheap or, even better, for free. Humans will accept almost anything if it is free. They will line up for hours to get a free drink with their coupon. They will purchase things they don't need if the sign says "buy one, get one free" and they will happily eat food they don't like if they don't have to pay for it.

Similarly people will spend hundreds of dollars at a "sale" if they think they are getting a bargain. Shops know this and have pretty much continuous sales. Sometimes the sales have a theme: Christmas, Mother's Day, Father's Day, end of financial year, start of financial year, stock run-outs, closing down sales (some businesses seem to be always closing down), door-buster bonanza sales and never-to-be-repeated sales.

Sales are often associated with mental illness and the concept of "crazy" bargains. This suggests the prices are so good that the people marking them down might have gone a little loopy. In fact some of the bigger sales also seem to put shoppers into a slightly psychotic frenzy in which they are happy to trample several fellow citizens to get 50 dollars off a fridge.

31. Apologising to the maid

All humans aspire to have someone else do their house and yard work. This is the only thing that keeps them sane. If you believe you will have to do this work for the rest of your life, you will go bonkers. Nothing good ever came from going bonkers.

Home helpers were once referred to as "maids", but this term is seldom used today as it is deemed to reinforce negative stereotypes. The exception to this is French maids, who wear skimpy cleaning outfits and have long legs. It is unclear whether these maids are very good at removing baked-on grime. They may exist purely for aesthetic purposes. French maids mostly seem to do dusting and flirting. They are almost never hired by women.

Unfortunately, most humans deep down feel guilty about someone else cleaning up after them and do not fully embrace the home help experience. Many people, for example, will clean their house before the domestic helper arrives so the cleaner will not think they are messy. There is good reason for this. Most cleaners are good at looking down their nose and making home owners feel bad about their sloppy habits. If owners are home when the cleaner is there, they will spend a lot of time apologising.

The thing cleaners hate most is windows. For decades it has been accepted that most cleaners do not do windows. They will happily brave toilets, sinks, laundry tubs and under the fridge, but windows are out of question. The reasons for this are not entirely transparent.

32. Inferiority complex

Deep down, all humans have an inferiority complex and a belief that they are missing out on something. When they visit the shopping centre, they just know that someone else is getting a better car park in some special, secret part of the complex that nobody has told them about. At the supermarket checkout, the other line is always moving faster. At the football, we all have to stand up during the good bits or we know someone else will be getting a better view.

In traffic, even when there is irrefutable evidence of gridlock, cars must keep changing lanes because they just know the other lane is moving faster. Some drivers will change lanes several dozen times leading up to a major snarl. Sometimes they create their own lanes off the side of the road in the apparent belief that there is another special lane just around the corner that the other 5000 cars in the gridlock haven't seen.

The trait begins in childhood. When children are given treats, they are always convinced that the other kids got more. They will line up the soft drinks side by side to ensure no one has even half a millimetre more.

Later in life they will become convinced that all their neighbours are richer than they are. They don't know how, but they suspect drug dealing or inheritance from a rich uncle. They also know that everyone else is getting better tax advice that will give them a huge windfall each year. Your accountant apparently knows about none of these deductions, so you end up paying more tax than anyone else.

And, of course, all the others have friends in the know who are on the ground floor of corporate floats where the shares open at 50 cents and are worth millions within weeks. They are the same people getting a big welfare windfall from the government, while you work for everything you get. At work, people just know all of their colleagues are getting paid more, even though they spend all day discussing sport and soap operas. And, of course, everyone else has a brother-in-law who is a builder/brickie/plasterer/plumber who will build their five-storey mansion for nothing and save them from the mortgage that you have to spend 40 years paying off.

If reality television has taught us anything, it is that most people are fairly ordinary and have the same fears, frailties, imperfections and insecurities as the rest of us. But you can only get on television if you know someone, which, of course, everyone does but you.

33. The weather obsession

Human beings are totally obsessed with the weather. They talk about it more than anything else. They predict it, they plan their lives around it, and everyone is an expert on it.

In particular, humans are obsessed with extremes of weather. They love bad storms, heavy rain that leads to floods, really hot days, really cold days, or weather that seems out of kilter with the time of year. Weather extremes give everyone something to talk about. You can meet a total stranger in the street and say: "Bloody hot, hey?" and you can be guaranteed that they will reply: "Bloody hot, all right". You can do the same with storms and rain. "Looks like rain," you can say, and you can be assured a "sure looks like it".

Some people have their own special ways of predicting the weather. Older people with gammy knees can feel the impending rain in their joints. Others look at the behaviour of birds and ants. Some people can smell impending rain. Others constantly check the radar on the internet or just look outside.

And, of course, when there are any extremities of weather, we are all convinced it is the worst that has ever been experienced. Generally, the television news crews can find an "old-timer" who can confirm this. On any hot day, during any flood, or after any storm, it is always possible to find an old-timer who will say the conditions are the worst he has seen in 30 years. This allows the television stations to declare a weather record. Human society loves a weather record. It confirms they have suffered more than anyone else in history and this gives them a great sense of satisfaction.

In fact, towns fight prolonged and bitter battles over weather records. The north Queensland towns of Tully and Babinda are in constant battle for the title as "wettest town in Australia". The west Queensland town of Cloncurry holds the record for the hottest temperature every recorded. However, this is always disputed by the town of Coober Pedy in South Australia, which claims the Queensland reading was taken inside a hot box.

The weather bureau used to be a party pooper when it came to declaring weather records. It would tell us it was just normal weather, or slightly above average. Now it plays the game and nearly always seems to manage to find a record that is being broken; something like the longest stretch since the 1950s of temperatures above 29 deg and humidity above 70 per cent. This makes us all feel better. We can safely say: "Yep it's a record one." "Bloody hot, isn't it?" "BLOODY hot. They say it's a record."

Of course, there is inevitably someone who will ring talkback radio disputing the record. They can always remember one really hot day during the Great Depression when the dam boiled and the bow-legged donkey they rode 300km to school just collapsed underneath them.

People equally want to be part of a record when the temperature is low. I was in Canberra in the winter of 1986 when it snowed at Parliament House for the first time in 30 years (or at least that's what the TV news said that night). I made many friends that day standing on the steps outside the building. People would walk past me and say: "Bloody great isn't it?" I retorted, quite cleverly: "BLOODY great."

During that very cold winter, the old hands of the Canberra Press Gallery would stand by the window stroking their chins in quiet reflection. "It's cold out there," one would say. "Too cold," another would add. "BLOODY cold," I'd contribute walking past, hoping to sound learned. "They say when it snows at Parliament House, governments fall," a wise counsel ventured. The government didn't fall, but the same could not be said for the washing on the line. It froze solid. The pegs fought bravely but the weight was too much. They groaned and popped and clothes crashed to the ground with the force of meteorites. I had to belt my work shirt with the hammer to get it soft enough to iron.

I have always liked to think of Mother Nature as being a bit like Alice, the housekeeper in The Brady Bunch: friendly, reliable and a bit grandmotherly. And most of the time she is. But catch her in a bad mood and she's an ugly piece of work. Alternatively, she may have time off every so often and leave her teenage children in charge of the weather.

During teenage weather we generally end up with storms and power outages. This is because power lines in Australia are mostly hanging off poles. During a storm they get hit by flying stuff and the power goes out. Sometimes the power does not go out completely but just becomes very weak. This is known as a brown-out. No one seems to know how brown-outs happen but they are frowned on. Nothing good ever came from a brown-out.

Confronted by a power-loss crisis, it is up to the man of the house to take charge. This initially involves rising to his feet and imploring everyone not to panic. Then he inevitably sets off with authoritative determination and walks straight into a wall. The next step is to go to the cupboard where the obligatory "big torch" is kept. Unfortunately, the obligatory big, square battery is often flat. If this happens, you need to find the candles, which will generally be located somewhere where they are almost impossible to find in the dark. You can also be almost guaranteed that the candles will be stored nowhere near the matches to light them. In fact, unless you are in a house with a smoker, you probably won't have any matches in the house at all.

Really bad storms tend to come with hail. Whenever it hails, it is very important that the size of the hailstones is compared with the relevant sporting ball. Hence, news reports usually tell us that a town was pummelled by "hailstones the size of golf balls". In fact, most times there is a hail storm we are told the hail is the size of golf balls. Curiously, when we see the pictures of the actual hailstones, they never really look that big. This could be because they have melted. Or perhaps they just look big when they are screaming out of the sky. Or perhaps the people giving the description don't play golf and they have no clue.

Occasionally, someone will break the mold and go with fruit and vegetable comparisons – like pea-size hail or orange-sized hail, which would presumably be like getting hit with cannon balls and would probably kill you. I once heard someone say their house was hit with hailstones the size of soccer balls. This would be like getting hit with a meteor. But it would keep the beer cold in the esky for many weeks.

34. The mini-bar

It is almost impossible for humans to sample anything from the hotel mini-bar without being overcome with guilt. The mini-bar sits in the corner of your room, calling to you like that freaky TV in *Poltergeist*. The next day, when you are checking out, you are always asked: "Did you have anything from the mini-bar last night?" While the hotel worker tries to ask this in a friendly tone, it nearly always sounds accusatory – as if you are trying to sneak out without paying for the tiny bottle of wine and the midnight Coke.

At this point, you always look a bit sheepish and say something like: "I just had a Kit-Kat because I was very hungry and didn't have any dinner." The hotel staff member instinctively gives one of those tisk-tisk looks and slowly enters the offending chocolate details into the computer. Then you look around to make sure no one was listening. "I was really hungry," you explain to anyone in the general area. "And was that all?" The hotel staff member asks with one eyebrow raised, knowing they have you on the ropes. "No", you finally admit. "I also had the little bag of nuts that cost $6 and the $12 Toblerone. Does my family need to find out about this?"

35. Smokers – public enemy No.1

Smoking was once considered cool. This was a miracle of marketing. Human beings were convinced they would be more attractive to the opposite sex if they had a piece of weed hanging out of their mouths and set fire to it. When this information was conveyed to the brain, the brain said: "That sounds about right." As previously established, brains are mostly clueless and cannot be trusted.

Slowly, as medical science gained ascendency over Big Tobacco, the tide turned on smokers. First they were told cigarettes blackened their teeth and gave them bad breath. Then they added poor stamina, ugly soot-belching and lung cancer. Eventually, smoking was declared responsible for everything from heart disease to bird flu. Next thing they will discover if you leave the thing in your mouth for long enough, your head explodes.

For adults who don't believe the research, or resist nicotine patches, smoking is a bit like being a classroom delinquent. When you took it up at school, you had to sneak out behind the amenities block to light up. Now, if you want to do it as an adult, you have to do the same thing.

Governments and companies have progressively restricted the area in which people can smoke. In fact, it is quite amazing how quickly smoking has gone from a widely embraced bad habit to a public nuisance up there with cane toads and drivers who wear hats. Smokers were fine when they were just killing themselves. Once we
found out their smoke was dangerous to the rest of us, we destroyed all ashtrays and headed for the smoke-free bunkers.

Once, when smokers went to a friend's home, they were greeted with matches and fancy lighters and everyone sat around apparently ignoring the thick cloud that prevented them from seeing one another across the room. Now the smokers are sent to sit on the back step with the cat. If the cat complains, they are asked to go home.

Smoking also once provided children with a sure-fire gift for most male members of the population – the ashtray. The ashtray was once an important contributor to the arts and popular culture. Children made them at school in pottery class and gave them to dads for Father's Day. There were singing ashtrays, statue ashtrays, portable ashtrays, giant ashtrays, precious stone ashtrays and plain black ashtrays that always smelled like a bonfire. It seemed that households could never have enough ashtrays.

Smokers were initially banned from lighting up in confined spaces like lifts and those little booths that take photographs. Then they added shopping centres, cinemas, trains, restaurants – anywhere that contained air, really. Now smokers huddle together outside buildings, shunned by fellow breathers and forced to stand inside some carefully-marked lines. If they step outside the line, they are often tisked by passers-by. This does not seem to worry them. Smokers eventually become totally oblivious to even the more severe of tiskings.

Children pass by and ask: "Mummy who are those people huddled together in that little square with smoke billowing from their heads?"
Mummy: "They're smokers, son. Don't go near them."

It is now widely believed that smokers go to hell. Heaven is inevitably a non-smoking zone.

There is talk of putting up "Warning, Smokers" signs in areas where the nicotine-addicted have been known to congregate. Eventually, the few left will be rounded up and sent to special smokers' colonies out west where there is a lots of spare air and the crops are all dead anyway due to drought and global warming. Alternatively, we may just establish a smokers' homeland where puffers can mix with their own kind and develop their own constitution and government. This new homeland would have a lot of ashtrays. This would help the smokers' homeland with their choice of birthday gifts.

36. Sport – nature's revenge

Champion golfer Lee Trevino astutely observed that when God made champion sportspeople, he always held something back. In other words, even the greatest players generally have at least one flaw that stops them from being unbeatable. Ordinary sportspeople generally have a lot more flaws. In fact, this is yet another example of the design defects in the human brain.

You would think that if you had served a few thousand times playing tennis and hit the perfect ace, the brain would store that information and just retrieve it next time you tried to serve. Alas no. As usual, the sporting files are a mess up there and apparently stored in different places. You have to get the information on the grip, the ball toss, the foot position, the angle, the swing and the target point from separate brain divisions. You can get a few of these areas to work together, but seldom the whole team. As a result, the thundering ace can easily be followed by a shot off the top of the racquet that ends up on the roof. The same is true for every sport. We have good days and bad days. If we do not practice, we forget a lot about how to play, and sometimes we get frustrated and break the equipment.

Different people have different expectations about their sporting prowess. Golfing champion Greg Norman used to talk about the days when everything went almost perfectly and he was in awe of himself. Former United States President Gerald Forde thought his golf game was improving because he was hitting fewer spectators. Dave Barry points out that playing sport is nearly always accompanied by an earnest-looking person telling you to bend your knees.

Golf is one of those games that demonstrate beyond doubt that humans like to punish themselves. It has been described as a six-kilometre walk punctuated by disappointments. The reasons for this are obvious. Golf requires you to take a tiny little ball and hit it with a tiny little piece of metal or wood at the end of a stick. This would be a whole lot easier if we could just use a bigger ball and a bigger stick. But, no, you can't do that. It is against the rules. Nobody ever knows where the rules came from or why you can't break them, but nobody ever questions them. In sport, the rules are the law – and you do not want to mess with that.

Part of the problem with sport is trying to prevent certain athletes from getting an unfair advantage. This primarily concerns drugs, or "prohibited substances", as they are generally known in sporting vernacular. To find these substances, sporting administrators have rigorous testing regimes. This means that when a great athlete wins a major event, they experience adulation, hugs, cheering crowds and fawning television interviews. Then they have to pee into a cup to make sure they didn't cheat.

Rules also have to extend to the types of equipment people can use and what they can wear. Sometimes, such as in swimming, this involves streamlined suits, caps and goggles. Tennis seems to have gone in the other direction. Female tennis outfits seem to be more about looking glamorous and creating new fashion labels. These also require a mysterious way to hide tennis balls.

Men, on the other hand, seem to have gone from the solid, streamlined and efficient tennis pants of the 1970s and 1980s to large puffy shorts that go past the knees. This is an alarming trend and the time has almost certainly come for tennis administrators to introduce random pants sampling to ensure oversized pants do not destroy the game or suck up large amounts of the world's fabric that could be used to clothe third-world families. It is quite possible that spectators only turn up at tennis matches to watch legs. Without legs, tennis could be in crisis.

On the flip side, it is also quite possible that that giant shorts could be restricting the careers of top players and reducing their ability to see out five-set matches. In big shorts, you have to run a few paces before the pants actually start to move, meaning you are running twice as far to achieve the same distance. If you are changing direction a lot, the pants can be two or three shots behind.

The other emerging crisis for tennis administrators is the rise of the grunt. The grunt is a loud, annoying noise that escapes from some players when they hit the ball. It can put the other players off, upset neighbours, scare small children and interfere with the laying habits of chickens. The top grunters register so high on the noise scale that they can drown out fireworks, aircraft noise and AC/DC concerts. Former Australian tennis champion Pat Rafter has blamed the grunting on uncomfortable underpants, and has devoted his retirement years to appearing in newspaper advertisements in comfortable jocks. In the advertisements, he smiles. This sends a subliminal message to the underwear-buying public that these underpants are indeed comfortable. "Otherwise why would Pat be smiling?" they logic.

Sport was designed for enjoyment, but it also comes with significant injury risk. In professional sport, the biggest injury risk comes from writer's cramp. This is particularly the case for Australian cricketers. Sure they will bat a bit, field some balls and bowl a few overs, but that is nothing compared to the memorabilia they will have to sign. Cricket memorabilia is created for every cricketing occasion. And they get it out quickly. If a bowler takes five wickets, by lunchtime the next day the host broadcaster is flogging 14,000 "limited edition" prints to remember the moment forever, all personally signed by the player.

When cricketers do their warm-ups, there is no longer arm stretches or star jumps. It is all about exercising the fingers to sustain a full five days of memorabilia signing. Talent scouts travel the country in search of promising youngsters who can remain at the crease for an autograph session for several hours. They also look for brash young writers who can make a quick breakthrough with large strident signatures delivered at high speed. It doesn't matter if you are making centuries or taking hat-tricks, if the writing hand sustains injury, you carry the drinks.

Cricket is a curious game that can only be understood in a small number of countries where humans are trained in its nuances almost from birth. During an Australian summer, a century (100 runs) from an Australian batsman is a bigger news story than elections, overseas disasters or major crimes.

The captain of the Australian cricket team has the most important job in the country after the Prime Minister and the Governor-General. In fact, I suspect if both those positions were vacant at any time, the cricket team captain would probably be next in line to run the country.

Australian captains generally stay in the role for at least five years, or until they stop making runs or become really unpopular. The ushering in of a new Australian captain is akin to the coronation of a new monarch. This only happens when you retire the existing captain. The retirement process takes forever because the captain must be farewelled at every cricket ground in the country. This mostly consists of putting them on the back of an open truck and driving them in circles. There is usually waving involved.

The main purpose of a cricket match is to produce statistics and break records. In every match, at least 20 records are broken and lots of new player statistics are created. Cricket has records for pretty much everything, like the most number of runs scored by an Australian player against India before tea in temperatures above 32 degrees Celsius.

Cricketers have to deal with the fickle Australian public who expect to win every match, and for players to always perform perfectly. When they are scoring lots of runs, the players are national heroes and important role models for young children. When they are not scoring runs, they are useless, lazy pork chops who should be ashamed of themselves. If Australia wins a match, it is proof that all is how it should be. When it loses, it is a national emergency. Everyone laments the "crisis" in Australian cricket, and they want to bring past greats out of retirement.

All the action in cricket takes about two seconds. Then you wait about a minute for the next two seconds of action. During that minute, the two seconds of action is replayed about 15 times. It is analysed by television and radio commentators who once played the game, and it is compared with a similar two seconds of action in 1964.

Umpires have the toughest job because they have only one second to make a judgement on whether during the two seconds of action anything actually happened. To do the job, umpires must be young, sharp and alert. Unfortunately, under the conventions of cricket, umpires actually have to be retired Sheffield Shield players from the 1940s and mostly have failing eyesight.

Another object of the game is to stand in a paddock for five days without being hurt by the dangerous, hard ball. When you are batting, you are given a bat to protect yourself. Players are also given a mysterious "box" to protect the "privates". The box is only ever discussed in hushed tones, and hidden in the bottom of large cricket bags. When the mysterious box fails to protect the privates, this causes considerable excitement in the television commentary box. They can generally relate it to a similar assault on the privates in 1973 during the golden era of fast bowling when no body part was safe. Players are sympathetic to the writhing victim, but actually look like they are fairly amused.

Commentators also occasionally talk about a batsmen "getting one right up in the blockhole". They never explain what it is, but it can't be pleasant. Nothing good ever came from getting something in the blockhole.

37. Computer games

It is hard to remember what life was like before computer games. Parents seem to believe that children in the past used to go to the creek and catch guppies or play in the mud when there was no PlayStation or Xbox. Most parents also seem to consider playing in the mud and catching guppies was a better way to spend time than playing computer games quietly in a clean room. They also concede that they would no longer let their children catch guppies or play in the mud in case they drown or get dirty.

While computer games were originally aimed at children, they are now played by all age groups. Many years ago, my wife bought me a Super Nintendo video game for Christmas to help me relax. Almost immediately afterwards my hair started falling out, my hands began to shake uncontrollably and I started putting my briefcase in the fridge.

Once I started the game, I became obsessed with it. Every spare minute I spent staring at the screen with a little control in my hand trying to jump ravines, king-hit little brown things with legs and avoid these incredibly annoying flying ducks.

The game, as I recall, seemed to be based on the adventures of Sonny Bono and his brothers who were on a journey somewhere to rescue a princess. Sometimes they got special powers. This made the journey easier. There was midget Sonny Bono, who had no special powers and whose head was not particularly good at smashing bricks. When this Sonny Bono brother ran into a mushroom, he became Super Sonny Bono, who was a bit bigger and had a much better head for wall demolition. When Super Sonny Bono ran into a funny-looking flower, he became Fireball Sonny Bono. This Sonny Bono was my favourite because he could shoot balls of flames that roasted those flying ducks before they sat on you. The final brother was Invincible Sonny Bono, who any of the brothers could become by running into a particularly agile star. Invincible Sonny Bono, as the name suggested, simply bopped aside anything or anyone in its path. He would have been very handy at the post-Christmas sales.

Despite its original intention, this game was far from relaxing. It was stress city. One wrong move and Sonny Bono or one of his brothers could be flattened by a fireball, eaten by a plant or walloped by a turtle. That's a big responsibility. The stress was heightened by the fact that every time I thought I had rescued the princess, a little smart alec so-and-so woman jumped out of a bag and told me the princess was in another castle. This woman obviously had no idea what I went through to rescue her out of her lousy bag. I told myself that if she kept this up, I would just pick her up and feed her to the plant.

For about a week I was stuck at a level in the game where Sonny Bono just seemed incapable of making a jump. He ran along the platform, I pushed button A and he splattered into the side of a cliff and disappeared into whatever abyss exists below the TV screen. Every time. For a while I thought Sonny was just tuckered out because of all the running and jumping I had been making him do. Then, in desperation, I decided I should read the instruction book for the first time. This taught me many enlightening things about stars, mushrooms and jumps. Beginner's tip: Read the instruction book BEFORE you spend a week jumping off the same ravine.

My son, who was three years old at this time, had not yet mastered the game but did a stylish commentary. When Sonny Bono fell off one of the cliffs he chimed in with: "Down the gully". When I slayed the dragon to rescue what's-her-name in the bag, he informed me: "Sorry Dad, but the princess is in another castle." Listening to me play, he also learnt some new words that we had to unteach him before pre-school.

The other problem with computer games is that once they enter a house everything else stops. There is no more cooking, cleaning or family meals. In my case, I stopped asking people about their day or whether they had any homework. The only thing I wanted to talk about was where you could find the extra bonus points, and which pipes had the secret passages. My only ambition in life was to finally rescue the princess.

Unfortunately the rescue did not happen. After about 10 levels of stressful adventures rescuing ungrateful women out of brown bags, I simply gave up. This was not easy. For a while it was just cold turkey and I craved the game day and night. I tried chewing gum and eating more. I took up reading and looked for creeks where I might find guppies. Eventually, I stopped having dreams about being chased by plants, and started asking people about their day again. Over time I even stopped putting my brief case in the fridge and remembered where I parked the car. For all I know, the princess is still in the castle waiting for me.

38. Fluff

While humans all have their individual pet hates, obsessions and idiosyncrasies, they share a common aversion to fluff. The fluff aversion transcends colour, religion, demographics and income. Everyone accepts that a piece of fluff on the shoulder must be removed.

Nobody is really sure what fluff is or where it comes from. It is generally a little white roll of something that somehow ends up on your clothes. This puts you at a significant disadvantage, because generally you cannot see the fluff but everybody else can.

You first become aware of it when the person you are talking to suddenly diverts their eyes to your shoulder and looks mildly uncomfortable. Over the course of a few minutes, the discomfort grows to full-blown disquiet. At this point they reach out with their hand and physically brush the fluff from your clothes.

Nobody ever asks permission to remove fluff. People are born with an innate belief that fluff removal is part of their birthright. And once they go into a full-blown fluff removal frenzy, they are well past the self-control stage needed to seek permission to invade your personal space.

Sometimes, if the fluff removal manoeuvre happens too quickly, your reflexes kick in and you may inadvertently slap the other person, or in cases of martial arts experts, knock them out cold or break a brick. This is not a big deal. It is regarded as acceptable collateral damage in the global war against fluff.

Curiously, it is unclear what happens to the fluff after it is removed. Rather than being carefully removed and disposed of thoughtfully, fluff is usually just flicked asunder to an unknown destination. The fluff almost certainly goes on to infect another unsuspecting human shoulder. It is entirely possible that there is only one piece of fluff on the entire planet but it keeps getting transferred in the flicking process.

39. Royalty

Humans have long been obsessed by royalty. They are particularly popular with women's magazines and people who once lived in England. Royalty gives us a connection to colourful histories when battles were fought and nations won and lost. In those days, royalty seemed to go completely mad a lot and get beheaded fairly regularly. Modern royalty often train in the military and learn to fly helicopters. Thankfully, in modern times, they are not regularly beheaded.

Alas, when members of the Royal Family are trained for their official duties, the courtier types always seem to forget the "how to pull the little string on the plaque" segment. Royal people really have only two tasks in their job descriptions – wave, and open things. Waving they do quite well – the result of thousands of years of breeding and an exhaustive wave-training regime that begins immediately after birth. But the average royal seems to have no clue when it comes to pulling the little string to expose the plaque. They always seem to pull the wrong one, requiring a special plaque-string consultant to sneak over and give them the right one or sometimes perform an emergency manual curtain string bypass.

Despite this inevitable false start, the crowd gets very excited when the curtain opens to reveal the plaque. "Well will you look at that," they think. "There's a little plaque behind that little curtain. I certainly wasn't expecting that. I will now clap very loud."

Rules of behaviour

40. Going up

Society is governed by a series of unofficial rules which we all follow without question, even though we do not know who set the rules or the consequences of breaking them. These include: Don't wear a Disney-character tie on a first date, don't wear denim at the opera, and never wear brown socks with blue trousers. It also pays to avoid being cheerful on Mondays. People hate that.

Some of our most stringent unwritten rules relate to standing in a lift. The most important of these is never look at anybody while you are in a lift. You can look at the floor or the ceiling, read the sign that advises you to avoid lifts during fire, and keep your eye on the little red light telling you what floor you are on. Just make no attempt to look at or in any way engage another human being.

The reason for this is that most human brains at some level are claustrophobic. This is because brains spend their days and nights trapped inside a confined skull. This can get to you after a while. The lift reminds the brain that it is trapped in a small space. By staring at the floor or the ceiling, the brain snaps into a funk that locks it into a total lift denial. As soon as you make contact or talk to another person, the funk breaks and the full horror of the lift is exposed. If you doubt this, just try hopping into a lift and staring at someone. They immediately get twitchy, go pale, perspire and usually leave the lift two floors before they meant to.

One of the scariest experiences in a lift is when you walk in and discover all the wall space is taken. This forces you to stand in the exposed ground in the middle. Here the protocols enter a grey area. You have a choice of either standing in front of someone with your back to them, or in the middle of the cubicle knowing everyone is scanning your back for signs of dandruff, moth damage or fluff. You can put your back to the door, but people who walk into lifts don't want to be greeted by a back. Nothing good ever came from being greeted by a back.

Another big worry is entering a lift with a pregnant woman. You just know it is going to break down mid-floor and you'll have to deliver the baby. All lifts should come with instructions on how to deliver babies. They should also come with an unread newspaper and hot water (I don't have a clue why, but I saw a movie once where a baby was born in the back of a taxi and the paper and water were considered vital).

Unwritten protocols also apply to train travel. For example, you never sit next to anyone if it can be avoided. There are good reasons for this. As someone prepares to sit next to you, you don't know until the last minute whether the posterior clearance required matches the seatage available. At that crucial moment of impact, there is a good chance you are going to be pinned helplessly against the window or flung full-throttle into the air by the sheer thrust of cushion displacement. When you're pinned in by a mass-mighty seatmate, Murphy's Law dictates that you will need to leave the train before the person blocking your path. This seldom ends well.

Sometimes, if you just agitate your body a bit before your station, the person will get the message and let you out (you can't actually talk to them – that's a serious breach of train protocol – but some grunting is allowed). Other times they just sit there and you are forced to use what little run-up you have to take a flying leap over them and hope you can make a soft three-point landing on the floor without impaling yourself on the inevitable umbrella in the aisle. At this point, your briefcase generally flies open and the crusts of the Vegemite sandwiches you took for lunch deposit themselves in the lap of a passenger in the seat opposite. You don't apologise. People who use public transport expect crusts once in a while.

Getting out of the train can be difficult even if you have the aisle seat – particularly if you are wearing a jacket and your seat buddy is partly sitting on it. In these cases you have two choices – the snatch or the clean and jerk.

The snatch involves throwing your body sideways in one mighty heave in the hope that the jacket comes clear and you can bolt for freedom. The danger with the snatch technique is, if you misjudge the weight of your seat companion, the jacket might rip in half and you could fly into a group of standing passengers – creating a domino effect which reverberates through several carriages.

A safer bet is the clean and jerk. Make a slight lean, take the slack and ease it out in one clean sideways motion. Some women react badly to this and hit you over the head with their handbags. This hurts, but is considered part of the normal risk associated with train travel.

41. Turning up

Filmmaker Woody Allen once famously remarked that 90 per cent of success in life comes from turning up (although the per cent he actually used seems to vary a lot when he is quoted). He may have even understated the percentage.

There was a time when humans were obsessed with winning. Remember when kids had to win something to get a trophy? Now they get them just for turning up. They all have cupboards full of trophies and certificates that proudly declare that they turned up for all manner of things.

In fact when future civilisations dig up 21st century civilisations, they will find mostly certificates. Millions of certificates are handed out each day to celebrate people winning stuff, doing stuff, finishing stuff and achieving stuff. But mostly they are for turning up. If you turn up for something you are entitled to a certificate. That is our basic right as a member of a society.

As a result of this, the average Australian child probably has 3256 certificates by the time they turn nine, and can accumulate enough in an average childhood to wallpaper an entire house. At school or sport presentation nights, most children walk away with folders full of certificates for everything from not failing too badly, to picking up rubbish, and breathing proficiently and regularly.

Of course certificates can never be thrown away. These must be kept for decades in case you need them one day. But so far there are no documented cases of anyone ever actually needing a certificate one day. The only exception to this is birth certificates. For some reason, people need constant proof that you were born. Standing in front of them just won't do it.

The tendency to celebrate turning up has now permeated high-level sport, even the Olympic Games. During the 2000 Sydney Olympics, everyone was very excited when local hero Cathy Freeman got the gold in the 400m sprint. But we saved the real excitement for a guy called Eric from Equatorial Guinea. Eric took what seemed like just under four hours to swim the 100m freestyle but heck, he turned up. It was the stuff of legends.

In golf, the reports always declare that Tiger Woods won, someone you never heard of came second, and Greg Norman turned up. Greg Norman doesn't win any more but he has mastered the art of turning up. He even calls press conferences to announce he has turned up.

Social pages are full of pictures of people who turned up at functions. It is as if people never actually expect anyone to turn up at their events. They call the photographers and say: "You've

got to get down here. A whole lot of people have turned up."
The next day the papers are full of happy snaps of smiling
people who turned up and look fairly happy about it.

Further evidence comes with programs like *Big Brother*. Once, if
someone turned up at your house and stayed for three months,
they might be thought a bit rude. But now you become a
modern-day hero and they give you a lot of money. *Big Brother* is
something of a national turning-up championship. And everyone
gushes at the great achievement. The family is proud. People are
in tears. There is talk of books, film rights and souvenir coasters.

The Royal Family are the masters of turning up. The Queen has
been turning up for years. In the months before she arrives
anywhere, the media is full of stories about the fact that she
plans to turn up. On the day she arrives, people celebrate in their
thousands that she has turned up. They all hope that one day she
might turn up again. In the meantime, she turns up somewhere
else.

42. Neighbours

It is very important to always be good to your neighbours,
because if anything newsworthy ever happens they will become
the prime source of information about you and your life. And
whatever that is, you can be sure the neighbours will be shocked.

At least 70 per cent of news reports about major suburban
events begin with the words: "Neighbours were shocked today
when they heard...". Neighbours seem to be shocked fairly easily.
They are shocked by shootings, Lotto wins, floods, fires,
robberies, and the fact that they have been living near serial
killers. And they seem to derive most of their impressions of
people from observing them wash their cars. This appears to be
the only time many people venture outside into the view of
neighbours. Apparently, even terrorists and organised crime
figures like to have a clean car.

NEWSREADER: "Neighbours were shocked today to discover the man who lived next door was wanted in three states for armed robbery, extortion and conspiracy."
REPORTER: "One neighbour, who declined to be named, said the man had kept to himself but once nodded at her when she went to collect the mail."
NEIGHBOUR (not her real name): "Certainly he gave no indication of shooting anyone or that extortion thing. I'm not sure what a conspiracy is but I certainly didn't see one of those. We certainly never expected anything like this to happen in our street."
REPORTER: "So would it be fair to say you are shocked?"
NEIGHBOUR: "Oh my Lordy yes."
REPORTER: "Just how shocked?"
NEIGHBOUR: "Very shocked. Yes, I would definitely say very shocked. Can I just add that he had a very clean car and I think he recycled."

While neighbours in Australia are often reluctant sources of news commentary, in America neighbours seem to consider it part of their constitutional duty. This harks back to the tradition of Paul Revere, who was so excited to find out first that the British were coming, he rode his horse to every house to spread the news. Within 10 minutes of any event in the US, the neighbour has usually isolated a suitable spot for a media conference, practised a 30-second grab, and hired an agent and printed souvenir T-shirts.

In modern times most people like to keep to themselves and adopt a "just enough" approach to their neighbours. They want to know their name and trust them enough to feed the dog during holidays, but they seldom want to watch the football together or do barbecues. There are good reasons for this.

The neighbour/friend relationship is one of the most difficult in any society. If you commit to the full socialisation schedule and then you discover you actually do not like them, the exit strategy is very complicated. In this situation the neighbours are hard to ignore and, short of selling your house, they will notice very quickly that the barbecue invitations have dried up.

At this point there is a very high risk of a full neighbourhood war. This generally begins with a dispute over a fence or a noisy stereo and ends with an appearance on the Jerry Springer Show, complete with an actual awkward brawl.

"Just-enough" neighbours are generally content with being on nodding terms. This is polite and safe and can seldom be misinterpreted. This can fairly safely be up-sold to a shouted weather remark like "bloody hot, isn't it?" On most occasions the neighbour will be in total agreement on the state of the temperature and will acknowledge with a "sure is". This loosely qualifies as a conversation with a neighbour and can generally appease any neighbour-neglect guilt for at least a few weeks.

Another source of angst between neighbours is the "keep an eye on the house while we are away" request. This creates a high-pressure situation. How are you supposed to keep an eye on it? Should you sit in your room with binoculars and watch it all day? How do you know if the person mowing the grass is meant to be there?

My family was once asked to keep an eye on the neighbours' house when they went overseas. When they got back, they had been robbed. It is hard not to feel guilty about this. It is probably a given that they did not think we had done particularly well keeping an eye on the place. Deep down, they might have even blamed us.

The stakes are perhaps even higher with the pet-feeding favour. This involves keeping an actual living thing alive for a week or two. This should be easy, but pets tend to fret when their owners are away and sometimes drop dead from stress. When this happens you can just replace them with a similar-looking pet from the store, but children tend to notice this. They don't generally believe that the pet looks different because you have looked after it so well.

43. The thin blue line marker

The real test of the seriousness of a crime is the reaction of "seasoned" police. If the crime is really bad, television reporters tell us that "even seasoned police were shocked". This is because any policeman who is seasoned has seen a lot of bad stuff. They don't shock easily. In fact they barely smile or change facial expression. If they are shocked, the crime is truly shocking. If they cry, they may be losing it. If they laugh, they may have already lost it. Inevitably the question will arise: "When does a policeman becomes seasoned?" I suspect this takes about 20 years. Less than 10 years they are still rookies, and between 10 and 20, they are only lightly seasoned.

Of course every media story involving police must come with a public interest message. When someone falls off a bridge the message is: "Be very careful around bridges." When someone drives into a pole after consuming too much alcohol, it is: "Do not drink and drive." When there is a murder, it is: "Police today urged citizens to avoid murdering anyone."

The other really important message is to swim between the flags. Australians are told pretty much from birth that when they are at the beach they must swim between the flags. Police and lifesavers repeat the message whenever they are interviewed in a beach setting. When you go swimming, the guy with the megaphone reminds you every few minutes to swim between the flags. The weather people on the news bulletins remind us about the flags, and there are signs everywhere prompting us to stick to the flags. You would think by now everyone would get it. But just in case: "SWIM BETWEEN THE BLOODY FLAGS, OKAY?!!"

Over the years, police have developed their own language to try to avoid talking to the public about crimes in plain English. In police speak, men are known as "male persons", suspects who are about to be arrested are "helping police with their inquiries" and pretty much everything they say is "alleged" rather than true. Offenders "abscond" rather than run away, stabbing someone is an "unlawful wounding", cuts are "abrasions", police cars "give chase" rather than just chase, and officers "have cause" to speak to people when they are "acting suspiciously". When they know who committed the crime but don't know where they are, they are known as a "person of interest". When the person of interest is caught they become a "suspect" while they are being interrogated and "the accused" when they are charged.

There is a common misconception that the hardest thing about police work is catching criminals. Equally hard is coming up with the name for a major police operation or a serial criminal. The problem dates back to the period of Jack the Ripper. This was considered such a good name for a criminal that the constabulary have been battling ever since to match it with names like the Granny Killer, the Postcard Bandit, the Yorkshire Ripper and the Unabomber.

Major police operations are even harder. In inspired moments they have come up with abstract gems like Operation Echo Shine. But on some days, despite extra manpower and the help of the big dictionary, they come up blank. This is a bummer at the press conference to announce the operation. "Ladies and gentleman, we have just arrested a major crime gang and destroyed 1000 hectares of drugs in a raid we called Operation Drug Bust," the Commanding officer would begin. "We know, this is a really lame name for the operation and we are deeply ashamed of it. We are standing down the guy who wrote it and there will be a full inquiry."

44. The full inquiry

Australian society spends a lot of its time having inquiries. In fact, pretty much every time anything happens, there must be an inquiry into it.

And no ordinary inquiry. It must be a "full" inquiry. People always call for a full inquiry. No one ever calls for a half-baked, partial or empty inquiry. It must be full. This seems to keep everybody happy. Sure, something bad has happened, but there will be a full inquiry. By the time the inquiry reports, no one can generally remember the incident that sparked it. There are lots of recommendations, which can generally be ignored.

Inquiries are society's way of killing time to allow us to get over or forget things. Of course, the golden rule of any full inquiry is that it must conclude that the whole system is a total debacle. People will expect and accept debacle as a suitable explanation for things going wrong.

"No wonder something bad happened," we all think. "The whole system was a total debacle. The full inquiry has saved us again."

45. Petrol station protocol

Petrol stations are full of helpful signs mostly designed to prevent you from blowing anything up. Unfortunately, human beings have erected too many signs and nobody actually reads them now. This is why life is so chaotic and sometimes things blow up.

Petrol station signs warn against using matches near petrol and allowing children to get out of the car and play with the petrol hoses. They also frown on using naked lights. I'm not sure what naked lights are, but they sound obscene and have no place at the family petrol station.

Petrol stations also frown on mobile phones. Mobile phones are frowned on practically everywhere. Many businesses and organisations seem to fear that mobile phones have a mind of their own and will infiltrate their electronic systems and run amok with their data. I'm not sure if there is any evidence of this happening but it is well worth having a sign just in case.

Another important sign at the petrol station warns you that it is a crime to fill up with petrol and not pay for it. It is lucky they tell us that. Without the sign, we would probably think the petrol was just a free service provided by friendly oil companies. The signs even tell us that trying to pay with a credit card that doesn't work is also an offence. This is quite stressful. Most people don't carry enough cash anymore to pay for petrol. This is because petrol bills now look like the national debt of small former Soviet republics, and people are scared to carry cash because they might be mugged or enticed to give it all to charity collectors or buskers.

I have been in petrol stations several times when people realise after they have filled up that they have left their wallet at home or their plastic card has malfunctioned, possibly due to a mobile phone running amok with their data. When this happens, it becomes a negotiation. Once the petrol is in the car, it is very difficult for the service station to take it back. Most often, the person is asked to leave something valuable behind as collateral while they go and get the money. I have seen people leave watches, spare tyres, bags of groceries and stuffed animals as surety. In one bizarre case, a father with a $30 petrol bill had nothing valuable with him and offered to leave his 10-year-old child there until he went and found the money. I'm not sure what he was thinking. If he didn't come back, was he expecting the service station to sell the child to an international slavery ring? If that was the case, isn't $30 a bit cheap? Perhaps the kid was bone lazy.

Another difficulty at the service station is understanding the protocol of where your car should point. There is never a sign for this, but at some garages there seems to be an unwritten rule that all cars must point in the same direction regardless of what side their petrol cap is on. If you spin around and face the opposite direction, it is like turning up at a black-tie ball in a safari suit. Generally, however, this is not a problem because there seems to be roughly the same number of right and left-side petrol cap vehicles. I assume there is some central controlling petrol-cap-side allocation authority that gives the sides to vehicle manufacturers.

There is also some mystery about how your petrol bowser is activated. Sometimes you stand there for ages waiting for it to spring into life. Other times it seems to see you coming. I think mobile phones might have something to do with this.

46. Making friends

Comedian Jerry Seinfeld says that by the time we turn 30 we have all our friends and "we are not taking on any new people". It is generally accepted that human beings need friends for their emotional nourishment and to borrow money from two days out from pay day. Friends are, however, quite hard work and in time-poor modern societies most people can sustain only a small number at any one time.

In fact, most surveys of the number of close friends people have suggest the number is between four and seven. This is less than half the number people stated 40 years ago in more sedate times.

What's more, the days of dropping in unannounced on people seem to be almost gone, with surveys showing most people now call ahead even if they are dropping in on their parents.

The friend drought might actually start earlier. While there are rare humans who seem to make friends with everyone, most people hang out with a relatively small number of people when they are kids, add a few during study or training, and then pick up one or two at work.

More recently, humans have come under significant friend volume pressure due to the growth of internet sites such as MySpace and Facebook. Most people have dozens of Facebook "friends" but only actually interact with a handful of them. In fact, most of their Facebook friends are people they met once (or not at all) and barely know.

Over the course of a lifetime, humans acquire different classes of friends depending on their age and social circumstances. Your first friendships happen soon after you can walk and talk, and grow from semi-structured institutions like playgroups and day care. Early in life, your expectations of friends are very limited. It is mostly about proximity. If someone is near you and happy to play with you, you figure they are your friend.

As you age and become more discerning, even children look for characteristics in friends that they might value, like tasty lunch to share or a common love of building blocks and rubber stamps.

By the time children go to school, they generally gravitate towards children with similar values and goals. This is when groups of like-minded people start to form, and these groupings often last throughout the schooling years.

School friendships are the most intriguing of all. Schools are contrived institutional environments in which people, who don't necessarily have any natural affinity, are put in the same uniform and encouraged to get on – often for up to 12 years. Over time, schools tend to produce a small number of very good friends and a large group of people you feel relatively comfortable with.

In fact, school friendships run so deep, most people can run into a school friend years after they move into adulthood and pretty much continue the same conversation. In contrast, you never forgive anyone who bullies you or treats you badly at school. You secretly hope they end up in a dead-end job and have nasty kids.

47. Pedestrian scrambles

Pedestrian scrambles are one of life's great miracles. People stand on four different corners, the light changes and they roar towards each other at breakneck speed. Logically the whole lot should just collide in the middle and fall like bowling pins. But somehow they just pass through – dozens of them – and emerge unscathed on the other side of the road. It's a bit like Arnold Schwarzenegger in Commando when 400 people with machine-guns are shooting but not one manages to hit him.

Pedestrian scrambles tend to bring out the competitive nature of humans. It certainly does with me. When I'm standing on the corner waiting for the little green man to appear on the light, it is important that I get to the middle of the road first. When I do, it gives me enormous satisfaction. I just know people all around me are thinking: "Look, he got to the middle first. That's really impressive." Sure they might feel bad for the couple of senior citizens that get jostled, but deep down they understand. We are humans. We like to get to places first. From early childhood we are taught that getting somewhere first is a good thing. Usually there are prizes.

With me it is not just about getting there first. It is also about doing it fast. When I was at school I always finished my work first. Sure it was written so fast that nobody else could read it (one teacher described it as "chicken scratch") but it was fast, and I was first and that had to count for something. Throughout my childhood, when I walked long distances with anyone, I tended to burn them off on the hills or just turn around and find I'd been talking to no one for a while. I lost friends that way, but at least no one fouled me as I was about to enter the stadium.

I also talked fast. At my high school presentation night I gave a 10-minute speech in about 45 seconds. When I sat down, the audience were all turning to each other asking: "What did he say?" The trouble with being a fast talker is that you spend most of your life repeating stuff anyway because nobody hears you the first time. This is good because it gives you the chance to change what you said if it did not come out right. It is the real-world equivalent of the radio station delay bleep button to cut out swearing and Ctrl z.

48. The other guy

Most humans have multiple personalities. This does not mean they have a mental illness. It just means they act differently in different situations. Jerry Seinfeld writes about night guy who goes out and has a big night, spending day guy's money and leaving morning guy to drag himself out of bed to face the day. When I walk the street, I am pedestrian guy, unashamedly stepping onto the zebra crossing and holding up cars just because I'm allowed to. I'm actually a big fan of zebra crossings because they help restore the power balance on a road to pedestrians. When I was a kid I would always walk bravely onto them in busy traffic. "Don't worry," I would assure those with me. "If anyone runs me over they will be in big trouble." How clever was that? (Luckily that was just kid guy and he later grew up and became far more cautious man guy.)

When I'm in my car, I'm driver guy, muttering under my breath about those bloody pedestrians on the zebra crossings. Some men go to a hotel and become outrageous pub guy, but go home later and be loving husband guy and father guy, even goldfish-feeding guy. They go to work to be competent employee guy, but go home and become useless washing-up guy or lazy-slob-sitting-in-front-of-the-cricket guy. We mostly don't like our other guys, but we learn to live with them.

49. The Garage

For anything to be credible in the human world it has to have started in a garage. Much of the world's creativity and enterprise seems to begin in the garage. Any rock band worth its salt needs to start as a garage band. And we constantly hear about really successful dot com and computer companies being started by two geeks in a garage.

This raises some fairly obvious questions like: "Why are the geeks in the garage and not just in the house?" What is it about grease and tools, old boxes of books, and broken cassette players from the 1970s that drives creative genius? We must be now coming to a point where new houses will include garages built purely for the purpose of housing musicians and geeks. Separate accommodation will be provided for vehicles. This will be known as the multi-vehicle room or car house, unless someone comes up with a better name while being creative in the garage.

This also raises the issue of where everyone is putting their cars. If garages are full of fledgling technology companies, emerging music stars and future internet millionaires, there is little scope for actual cars. These are just left on the street for birds to poop on. A pooped-on car is never a good look, particularly in a car yard. Prospective buyers will think: "Perhaps this car is not any good. If it was any good, why did that bird poop on it?"

50. Party music

One of the curiosities of so-called networking functions is that the music is nearly always too loud to actually talk to anyone. By the end of the night your voice is shredded from shouting and you have an overwhelming desire to find a quiet corner and assume the foetal position.

In fact, loud music has a lot to answer for in Western culture. Nearly half of all marriages that started in the 1970s have subsequently ended. I blame this on disco and the Bee Gees. Most 1970s couples met at discos and didn't really have any actual conversations because they couldn't hear anyone. They couldn't really see each other either because of the dark rooms with red and blue flashing lights. As a result of this, many couples were well-and-truly married before they realised they had nothing in common or didn't actually like each other.

Loud music is also responsible for many neighbourhood quarrels. As people pack tighter and tighter into our burgeoning cities, their stereo speakers are getting closer together. At the same time, walls are getting thinner and musical options are diversifying. The unhappy end result is that most people spend a lot of their lives listening to their neighbour's favourite music that they inevitably don't like.

This results in them thumping on walls to create the only sound widely regarded as more annoying than really loud music you don't like. Curiously, no one ever respects the musical tastes of others. It is never: "I don't like your music but I respect your right to listen to it." Rather it is: "I really hate your music and you are a complete moron for playing it and liking it."

51. Fine print

For reasons no one can understand, humans have created a whole lot of rules about everything. But they are okay with these rules being recorded in writing so small that nobody can read them. It is all about them being there.

In most cultures, the laws of the country are contained in volumes at least 50cm thick. Not knowing a law exists is not considered a valid reason for breaking it. This, by definition, means we are actually expected to know every law contained in thousands of volumes. This is why many people think it is easier to make an insanity plea.

When you enter most car parks there is a sign at the entrance with the conditions of entry. Most car parks have about 30 conditions and these are written in type so small that you would have to get out of your car and put your head within 20cm of the sign to have any chance to reading them. Of course, if you do anything wrong you are expected to know all of these conditions and they will throw the book at you.

Similarly, when someone wants to put a 40-storey building in a suburban area, they must put a sign out the front warning the neighbours that their quiet street is finished. These signs inevitably talk about parishes and counties and a whole heap of legal gobbledegook. When the bulldozers come in a few months later and people start to protest, the authorities protest: "Didn't you see the sign?"

In advertising, fine print is a bit like the conscience of the advertising message. It sits below most ads coming clean on what the message really means. Unfortunately, fine print by its nature is fine. It can never compete in size or dominance with the main message.

Hence we see "100% OFF SALE" in big letters and in tiny letters below we read "the above message may be bulldust".

Fine print tends to work okay in print because you can bring out the magnifying glass and actually read it. On television it is a lot harder. There are hundreds of images, loud voiceover people talking about "crazy bargains" and "buy now and pay nothing for 10 years". But on the bottom is all this tiny white writing that you can't read fast enough. Sometimes it seems to say "conditions apply". This could mean anything. It might mean "it's really cheap but you can't have any", "offer only available to Slovenian monks wearing black" or "sorry, only one in stock".

The other most popular fine print is "simulated demonstration". This means "what you see on screen is not actually happening".

In other words, batteries don't have arms and legs, cars can't drive across water, and the laboratory on the screen working night and day to create a better dandruff formula might not actually exist.

In vehicle ads, a popular fine print message is "foreign model shown". This presumably means that the car that is being advertised may not be available to you. Or it could mean that you can buy something that vaguely looks like this in your country but do not expect it to drive up the side of mountains, and it may get bogged if you drive it in the creek. The GPS tracking device might also talk to you in a foreign language.

52. Extras

Humans seem remarkably willing to accept extra charges on almost anything. In America and some European countries, tipping is considered compulsory. This involves paying for something and then paying extra for someone to actually give it to you. Tipping works okay for someone in a tipping culture. They seem to know how much to give. Australians, on the other hand, have grown up in a culture where service workers are generally paid okay and tipping is optional for someone who did a really good job, or if you don't want a whole lot of coins rolling around in your pockets. As a result, Australians travelling overseas generally get tipping totally wrong. This can mean losing your luggage a lot, being dropped off at the wrong sport and receiving odd-tasting food.

In Australia, many service companies leave a little place on the bill where you add "gratuities". Most people do not know what this is for and either leave it blank or write something like "yes please" or tick it. The tick does not actually mean anything. People tick because they think the bill is asking if they received their gratuities. Because most people do not know what they are, they assume there have, indeed, been gratuities. Ticking the section makes them feel good about this. Restaurant staff just shake their heads and make a mental note to sit you next to the toilets next time you come in.

Also in Australia, on most professional or service bills a bit is added at the end for "incidentals". We pay this even though no one really knows what incidentals are. The dictionary defines incidentals as "things that happen with something else". This does not really tell us much. If we query this, the incidentals are generally explained as "little expenses that happen along the way". This does not really tell us much either. What we really need to know is what are these little expenses and why are they happening along the way.

Other bills have an extra charge for "sundries". Sundries is an equally mysterious word. In cricket they are runs you don't have to score. On bills they appear to be a bit extra to make the amount look respectable. Or perhaps they are the things you pay for that the company does not have to provide.

When you order something through the post, they put some extra on to cover "postage and handling". Postage you can understand. That is the cost of sending it. But what is this handling? Who is doing all the handling? Are they taking your product and passing it around the office so everyone can handle it? Why does this handling cost so much? Wouldn't it be better if everyone kept their grimy hands off it and just put it in the bag and charged you less?

53. You have been placed in a queue

One of my favourite movie lines comes from the film *Small Soldiers*. In one scene, the teenage hero is on the phone to a toy company to report that their toy action figures have come to life and are running amok through a suburban neighbourhood. He is put through to a particularly annoying customer service representative who is absolutely no help. "Can't you put me through to a machine?" he cries in desperation.

Tall People Don't Jump

Generally, being put through to a machine is far easier than finding an actual human. In most cases, companies, government departments and organisations will expect us to deal with many layers of recorded machines before they will let us talk to any humans. In fact, nobody really wants us to ever get through to a human. They will give us all the reasons we don't need to talk to a human, confuse us with hundreds of options and menus and, if we are still impertinent enough to expect human contact, they will leave us waiting for up to an hour. The person we eventually speak to usually sounds like a machine, is based in a foreign country and has English as a third language.

During the long wait for a human, we are informed that we have been placed in a queue. Unfortunately, we do not know where we are in the queue. We might be two from the front, or in the line that stretches around the corner. If we are in the long line, the machine speaks to us several times to let us know we have not been forgotten. "Your call is important to us," the machine assures us. Then it tries to talk us out of waiting. "Did you know you can do most things on the internet?" it suggests. These days, everybody wants us to go to the internet to avoid talking to us. Of course when you get there you cannot do anything without a password. Most people who regularly use the Internet have an average of 50 different passwords to access everything from online banking to ticket sales. They can remember approximately none of them. And generally you cannot sign up to do any transactions on the internet without your account being activated. To do this you have to ring the customer service number. When you do this you are placed in a queue.

Early phone message machines were based just on pushing buttons for different functions. More recently, some companies, particularly banks, have introduced voice recognition technology. The concept is sound in theory. Tell the machine what you want rather than push a button. Unfortunately, the machine seems a little hard of hearing and apparently only understands you if you speak in a foreign accent. And the whole thing takes at least twice as long as the old push-button method.

And you don't really know what to tell it. You ring with a complicated business or banking question and it asks: "Please tell me what service I can help you with today?"
And you say: "Well it's a bit complicated. You see I really need to find out ..."

"I do not understand your request," the machine interrupts. "Please tell me what service I can help you with today." "Of course you don't understand it," you say fairly politely. "I was really just trying to tell you..." "Okay," it interrupts again. "I'll put you through to phone banking." "No, no, I don't want ...."

Too late. The voice machine has now sent you through to the phone banking machine. You only have three options, and none of them is good. So you hang up and phone the voice machine back. This time you are smarter. In your best foreign accent, you say: "Customer inquiry." "Okay," the machine responds, increasing your expectations. "I'll put you through to phone banking." "No, no, no, no! Not phone banking. Anywhere but phone banking! There is nothing at phone banking that can help me! Please don't send me back to phone banking!"

But it's too late. You are already being walked the green mile to phone banking with its three options and inflexible monotone conversation. You are locked in a terrible maze of buttons and options, account identifiers, biller codes, customer reference numbers, receipt codes with 400 numbers, extra security information, and pressing that rotten hash key. Once you are there, there is no way out. But it doesn't really matter. By then you will probably have no recollection of why you phoned and there will be nothing else they can help you with today.

Oddities

54. Out of rhyme

The biggest oversight when the English language was written was the failure to include enough words that rhyme. The founding language fathers clearly did not envisage poetry or modern song lyrics. As a result, most words only rhyme with about four others, causing significant distortions in literary imagery.

For example, love has nothing to do with a dove – but the two words are forever connected because they rhyme. And the moon will forever be associated with June, even though it is also in the sky all the other months.

Eventually poets threw their hands up and started using things like free verse and blank verse in an ill-fated bid to prove that real poetry did not need to rhyme. Nobody actually believes this. And eventually song writers gave up completely, culminating in the immortal *Tutti Frutti* with the deeply moving opening line: Wop-bop-a-loo-mop alop-bom-bom Tutti Frutti, aw rutti.

The trouble with rhyming poetry is that there is a fine line between art and just really bad lines that are contrived to rhyme. Often the worst of these happen at weddings when the happy couples write poems for each other. This whole process relies on love being blind, and mostly deaf. In the fairy dust of the wedding ceremony, these poems sound beautiful and romantic to the couple, and excruciatingly twee to everyone else. After about two years of marriage they also start to sound excruciating to the couple, and that part of the wedding video is quickly erased.

The other really worrying poetry is rhyming poetry written by people with little talent, who nevertheless believe it is brilliant. These people often read their work in public places and enter it in contests. People tell them their poems are good because they don't have the heart to break the truth.

These poems generally sound something like this:
I was walking past the sunny trees
When I fell over and hurt my knees
I got right up and I started to walk
And that night for dinner was pork

In music the rhyme is less important because, if you run out of rhyming words, you can just keep repeating the same line. For this to work it generally needs to be a good line with some catchy music behind it, like that song – "It's got to be perfect" by Fairground Attraction. This line was apparently a bit short, so they had to stretch the words. The word "be" became "beeee, eeee, eeee" and perfect also stretched to "peerrrfect". Nobody seemed to notice. The song was a huge hit. I have never heard of Fairground Attraction again. I think they might have run out of rhyming words.

55. Kaput

There is something particularly exciting about getting mail. No matter how old you get or how much mail you have received in your lifetime, when something arrives in that little box on your front fence, it is a very special thing. Of course, these days most mail consists of bills, notifications of mysterious lotteries you might have won, and personal letters addressed to "The householder". This doesn't really matter. It is really about the anticipation. Mail IS like a box of chocolates. You never know what you are going to get (and, in the case of chocolates, you need to get in early or you end up with the hazelnut crunch). Ben Elton, in his book *Stark*, reasoned that the thrill of mail was probably linked to childhood mail which tended to be associated with special occasions like birthdays and Christmas and cheques and cards from grandparents.

As a journalist, you get all sorts of interesting mail. Most of it (believe it or not) is positive – people saying they liked something you wrote, or seeking more information, or just wanting to tell you something. You do get the odd one accusing you of conspiracies with groups you've never heard of.

There's also the mystery mail, particularly at Christmas. Most years I receive at least two Christmas cards which are totally blank. I figure some very shy people must send them. For years I received a card from someone in the United States who signed it "your friend" and wrote like he'd known me all his life. I'm fairly sure I had never met the guy or even heard of him, and there was never a return address.

I have always regarded the mail system as some sort of miracle. You put something in an envelope then stick it in a red box and most of the time it arrives where you intended. Mind you, I regard most aspects of life as minor miracles. I never really believe the car is going to start and I certainly never expect the stereo to react when I touch the remote control. By never expecting much from anything, you can get pleasantly surprised a lot. Expect a lot and you spend most of your life disappointed.

Most humans, unfortunately, do expect a lot and seem genuinely outraged when things go wrong. Usually they blame the government. Governments are expected to make sure nothing ever goes wrong. If anything goes wrong, the government has clearly stuffed up and heads should roll. This is true if the power fails (blame the government, not the storm), the trains are late (disorganised government), there are floods (blocked government drains), interest rates go up (not enough government control) and jobs are lost (too much government control).

As a result of the expectation that nothing must ever go wrong, all western societies are awash with laws and regulations passed by politicians who have to be seen to be doing something after something goes wrong. Politicians are not allowed to say: "Shit happens". They are expected to pass laws that prevent shit. As a consequence, society is constantly tied up in red tape and unnecessary laws. This is also the fault of the government.

This approach ignores the obvious fact that in the human world things were never actually meant to work. In fact, I am fairly convinced that "kaput" is the normal state of being. If things were really supposed to work, we wouldn't have so many fix-it people like mechanics, doctors, dentists, repairers, lawyers and tradesmen. The whole world economy revolves around things not working and people keeping themselves busy trying to make them work temporarily before they return to their normal broken, ill or disputed state.

If you think about it, if it was normal for things to work, that would be the default position. Nothing would wear out. It would just get better. Cars would never break down. They would return to their normal state of working. We would not need any laws because everyone would naturally do the right thing. In such a society, police would merely exist to give directions and sell tickets to the Policemen's Ball. Lawyers would just do conveyancing and wills. In fact, if kaput was not the normal state of being, humans would not age and die. The harsh reality is that, from the time we are born, our biological clock is ticking. And the bloody thing never works properly.

56. Vending machines (no, the other ones)

If you ever need proof that nothing really works, try getting a stuffed toy out of those glass-box coin booths with the crane-like snapper claws. I've invested hundreds of dollars into them in the course of my lifetime and the only return has been a small blue elephant which fell down when someone accidently knocked the machine. This is particularly troubling for fathers. When my son was very young I used to be his number-one hero until he watched me try to grab him a stuffed Fred Flintstone out of one of those machines. Very soon he had dropped me for Porky Pig.

I suspect these machines have ruined the reputations of fathers across the world. I think they are also responsible for a large number of nervous breakdowns and family poverty crises.

There is no particular logic to ever using these machines. They are designed to activate the same area of the brain that compels people to gamble. It is about the thrill of the hunt and the possibility of winning. People tend to ignore the fact that you are investing a dollar each time to try to win a stuffed toy with a value of about 70 cents. It is even more mysterious in the case of machines with those tiny chocolates. You would be far better off just going to the supermarket and buying them. But there is no fun in that.

Clever machine owners generally fill their machines with a heap of cheap rubbish and two apparently expensive items like watches. The watches are probably super-glued to the machine. I have never met anyone who has managed to snare an expensive gift with the machine claws. In fact, the machine claws appear totally inept at grabbing things, again proving the theory that nothing really works.

57. Passwords

The spread of the internet has created enormous opportunity to perform all manner of tasks online. Unfortunately, to do this we require passwords. The average person now has somewhere between three and 50 passwords and can remember approximately none of them.

When passwords first came into use for electronic identification, we just used our date of birth and the names of our children. After a while this became the electronic equivalent of putting a key under a mat. It was the first thing hackers tried when they wanted to steal your identity.

To avoid this, passwords had to become more complex and harder to remember. There needed to be letters and numbers, some capital and some not. We needed to avoid any word that might be associated with us or anything we might have any vague chance of remembering ourselves.

To remember all of our passwords, we need to write them down somewhere that is easy to find. Unfortunately, this is the first place hackers look when they want to steal your identity.

58. Nicknames

Humans are given names by their parents at the time of their birth, or soon after. This is a major concern, because at this point in their lives humans can have no effective input into their names. Often significant damage has been done as a result of these names before they are old enough to understand the affliction.

Parents go through a multitude of processes to choose a name. Sometimes they pay homage to a grandparent or an actor they liked in a 1950s film. Celebrities often name their children after plants or natural objects. This is usually a result of drugs.

Different cultures have different numbers of names. In most western civilisations people have three names – a first name, a last name and a middle or "spare" name. The spare name is there in case of naming emergencies or identity verification.

In my case, my parents activated my spare name immediately. I was born Bevan Shane Rodgers. My parents (and everyone else) have always called me Shane. This was quite deliberate because Shane Bevan didn't sound right. A naming emergency clause was invoked and I became a Shane.

This seems like a pretty basic thing, but I doubt there have been more than a few days in my 50 years of life when it hasn't caused confusion. Every year at school the teacher called me the wrong name for the first week. Cold call sellers who have my full name from some mailing list always ask for Bevan (I just tell them there is no one there by that name). There is also an extraordinary amount of "official" mail that comes addressed to our full names. Cheques made out to "Shane Rodgers" need a full explanation before you can deposit them into a Bevan Shane Rodgers bank account. And so it goes on.

Some people who do not like their names just change them. This was once very common among celebrities. Most trivia buffs know that Marilyn Monroe was born Norma Jean, Elton John was Reginald Dwight and John Denver was Henry John Deutschendorf. Singing star Prince has changed his name a lot for no apparent reason (or perhaps to attract attention). He started off calling himself Prince. At some stage after that he changed it to the symbol O(+>). For obvious reasons, most people found this difficult to pronounce. As a result, he was generally referred to as The Artist Previously Known as Prince and sometimes The Artist. I think he may now be called Prince again, but nobody actually cares.

For a long while, most women changed their names when they got married (taking their husband's surname). This still happens a lot but is less common. There is also a big growth in hyphenated names as people try to recognise their new partner's name but preserve their family heritage. This is okay until their children marry other people with hyphenated names and they end up with a name so long that it no longer fits on invitations, and no one invites them anywhere.

Of course, after a while, names start to become irrelevant because other humans feel the need to rename their friends and colleagues. The reasons for this are not entirely clear. Sometimes it is just laziness. People take a long name and make it shorter.

Sometimes it is ironic. All red-headed men are pretty much called Bluey. Quiet people usually get called Rowdy, and scrawny people cop Muscles.

Sometimes nicknames are extraordinarily long for dramatic or comic effect. A friend at school was named Scott. His nickname was Ellymayclampersaurusshellpsychodemius (pronounced Ellymayclampersaurusshellpsychodemius). Eventually this was shorted to Elly. Adding a "y" is probably the most common and laziest way to make a nickname. Hence the world is full of people called Smithy or Jonesy.

Sometimes nicknames have been around so long people cannot remember their origins. Sometimes they are the result of "official" nicknaming of certain real names. William is Bill, John is Jack, Charles is Chuck, Elizabeth is Betty (go figure), Diana is Di and Richard is Dick (generally without much enthusiasm).

Very cool people get the rare nickname privilege of being known as just the first letters of their first and last names. Having a surname starting with "J" is particularly useful in this regard. Initial names like CJ, BJ and AJ always seem to work well. Most people like these nicknames because they sound cool when you say them and you hope some of the associated coolness will rub off on you.

People also have their porn star names. This is the name they would be given in the unlikely event of them becoming a porn star (possibly the ultimate naming emergency). There are varying versions of this, but the most common seems to be that your first name as a porno star should be the name of your first pet, and the last name should be the name of the first street you lived in. When most people try this, it turns them off this type of acting.

Recent years have seen the advent of the cyber name. On the internet, people seldom sign onto anything as themselves, fearing others will find out what they are really like or steal their identity. Instead they create a cyber name that allows them to roam the online world in total anonymity. These names are sometimes a full sentence and often say something profound about the owner, such as "this person cannot spell very well".

59. Beeping

What genius decided that machines should be taught to beep at us? The beep is the worst noise ever invented. Nothing good ever came from a beep. When you drive into a car park, you know you have to push the little green button and take your ticket. But the bloody machine still goes BEEEP, as if to say: "Take the ticket, you moron". Car park machines are always in a bad mood. I don't think they have a very interesting life.

Smoke detectors beep when you cook the toast, cars beep when they go backwards and also if you don't put your seat belt on, and they go beepzoid like a stepped-on cat when you try to lock them with a door still open. I think all beeps should be immediately replaced with the Tarzan jungle cry. This would be slightly less gnawing. But be careful because it may attract elephants. And Jane.

60. Nails on the blackboard

When mad scientists in science fiction stories make dangerous monsters, they usually give the monster a flaw or a weakness. This is because the monster usually goes bananas and tries to kill everyone. This cannot be allowed to happen. It isn't much of a story if the monster just kills everyone.

The human brain has been similarly wired in case it also goes berserk and runs amok. Its weakness is fingernails on blackboards. As soon as fingernails are run across a blackboard, the brain goes into a flap and vital organs start to shut down. The same effect can usually be achieved by running a rake over concrete or running rough metal against rough metal.

It seems that nature has built all manner of checks and balances into the system to prevent anything being unstoppable, and to help living things survive. For example, if you put a myxomatosis virus through a rabbit population, a small percentage survive. When AIDS went through the Boston prostitution community in the 1980s, a percentage of prostitutes did not get infected.

The same applies in the broader sphere. Somehow we seem to have enough people to do just about every job. While most of us would hate to work in sewerage works, some people love it. People clean toilets, work in the middle of the night, serve debt notices and get abused all day, kowtow to annoying people, cut people open and retrieve rotting bodies from the bottom of rivers.

People join the armed forces to get shot at. Others deliver mail in the desert, cut up dead animals, drive trucks all night, and work in factories performing the same task day in and day out. A recent online survey rated worm taster and animal sperm collector as the two worst jobs. These were rated slightly above flatulence analyst. Sometimes people do seemingly dull or smelly jobs out of necessity, but a surprising number really like what they do. It is as if a special area of their brains has been wired to believe that dirty or mundane work is their calling.

Perhaps nature has a greater plan to ensure species survive disease and all the bad jobs get done. If not for this, society would cease to function or get clean. We would have to force people to do the work by threatening nails on a blackboard.

61. Superman syndrome

Humans are slightly obsessed with super heroes because deep down they like the idea of someone rescuing them when they are

Tall People Don't Jump

in a heap of trouble.

Super heroes generally need two things – super powers and an alias so they can work among mere mortals with nobody noticing. In the super hero world, if you just wear a pair of glasses that is a sufficient disguise. No one ever expects that someone with glasses can leap tall buildings in a single bound. But they will ask if you can fix the problem with their computer.

Curiously, not all super heroes have super powers. Some just have a lot of money and spend time in the gym. Batman, for example, is really just a rich guy with a boomerang. He also has a decent car, a useful utility belt and a side-kick called Robin who mostly walks up the side of buildings instead of using perfectly serviceable doors.

The Flash is really fast and can get to the scene of a crime really quickly. He can't do a whole heck of a lot when he gets there, but he can certainly get there really quickly.

The most famous super hero is Superman. He has the whole deal when it comes to powers – super strength, speed, x-ray vision, heat vision and the ability to fly. Unfortunately, when Superman is exposed to a mineral called Kryptonite he turns into a ball of jelly. And the bad news for him is that everybody knows about the weakness because they have read it in the comics. This means that when the chips are down and all seems lost, Superman flies in with his cape and tights to seemingly save the day.

"Yah," people think. "Superman has arrived with his tights and super powers and stuff. Everything will be okay." But then the villain pulls out the Kryptonite and Superman turns into a pool of jelly. "Bugger," people think. "That didn't really work, did it?"

As the story goes, Superman is fairly ordinary on his home planet of Krypton, but on Earth he has extraordinary ability.

This type of syndrome also happens in the real world, particularly with French-speaking men. In the movie *Simply Irresistible,* the French restaurant guy explains that in France he is just another man. But as a French-speaking man in America he attracts attention, and women. In America he is Superman.

Most foreigners have a similar experience. In their home countries they can be ordinary and dull, but abroad they are interesting and exotic. Humans are always impressed by exotic things. They figure that if someone or something is from a different part of the planet, they must be better than local things. This is almost never the case. But, just to be sure, hundreds of thousands of people travel abroad each year and bring back a suitcase of exotic things, generally made cheaply in another part of the world (that they didn't visit) utilising efficient sweat shops. People also find that when they are among a whole lot of foreigners for a while, they no longer seem too exotic or interesting. Then these people go home and tell their friends and neighbours what an interesting and exotic time they had. Sometimes there are slide shows.

Getting around

62. Behind the wheel

At some point in human evolution our brains decided our bodies did not move fast enough. Sure we could walk or run, but with so many places to go and people to see, it just wasn't enough. For a while we turned to horses to get us there faster. Humans and horses proved a very successful combination for land travel and the making of John Wayne movies. Horses even had their own brains and expected little more than some chaff, water and a bit of mane stroking. Horse transport seemed like the perfect solution to the slow human body.

Alas, we got greedy. "Sure, horses are fast and only expect

chaff," we said. "But now we have even more things to do in our limited 24 hours a day. We need to go faster." At first trains seemed to be the solution. They could go very fast and carry a lot of people. They also had very cool horn-whistles that went off when you pulled a little rope. Whole generations of young men aspired to be train drivers just so they could pull on the little rope.

Alas, we got greedy again. "Sure, trains are fast and carry a lot of people," we said. "But they have to go on tracks. What if the tracks don't go where I need to go? We need something else. We need the automobile."

From that day, everything about human civilisation changed. The automobile, or car, became an extension of the human body. The car became a great leveller. Meek and skinny people who had sand kicked in their face on the beach (unless they used a Bullworker) could buy a big car with a bull bar and intimidate other drivers on the road. Rich people who wanted to flout their wealth could buy an expensive vehicle with leather seats, packed with extra features they never used. Wealthy middle-class families could buy expensive all-terrain four-wheel-drive trucks to drive their children to pre-school in the suburbs. Teenagers could adjust their cars so they made a lot of noise and really annoyed people.

With cars, came "tinkering". Only men tinker with cars. Tinkering involves lifting the bonnet of a car and pushing, twisting and tightening things. Some men who know what they are doing tinker to make their cars go better. Most others have no idea what they are doing and just tinker to prove their masculinity. Sometimes people acquire a vehicle purely for tinkering purposes. These vehicles tend to sit in backyards for several years, sometimes decades, because the male of the household plans to "do it up one day". Doing up a car generally means making it drivable and capable of taking its place among other actual cars on the road. For much of the 20th century, doing up a car was an aspiration of most suburban males. Few ever achieved it, but they kept the dream alive with tinkering and backyard cars. Eventually the backyard cars became home to snakes. Once this happened, the tinkering ended.

The great dream of the automobile was for humans to go wherever they wanted, fast and uninhibited by natural limitations, horse chaff availability, or rails. In a car, a man could be free. He could drive forever on the open road, wind in the hair, music on the radio, attractive woman in the passenger seat.

Alas, everyone else had the same idea. And, while the car could go places without rail, it generally needed roads. As a result, millions of people ended up on the same roads going to the same places at the same time. This meant cars ended up spending most of their time going slower than a person could actually walk. This caused a lot of frustration, and the invention of a human condition known as "road rage". Road rage involves getting angry at just about everybody else on the road because they are on the road and preventing the wind going fast enough to get into your hair. Car manufacturers dealt with the road rage problem by inventing car horns. Horns do not solve congestion problems, but they give you something to do with your frustration while you are waiting for the traffic to move.

Comedian George Cailin observed that, when you are driving, everyone going slower than you is a moron and anyone going faster is a maniac. This default position gives people plenty of reason to use their car horns. The big problem with car horns, however, is that they generally have a one-sound-fits-all design and often exaggerate the message you are trying to convey to a fellow motorist or pedestrian.

For example, when someone walks out in front of you and you are in a fairly positive frame of mind you want your horn to say: "Excuse me mate, that's a bit dangerous. You might want to look first next time." But no, the horn gets carried away. "Get out of the way you stupid jerk," it shouts. "What are you? A complete idiot? Your mother wears army boots and your father is a pansy." People naturally react badly to this type of horn attitude, and road rage can result.

Road rage is potentially very dangerous. Once human beings are attached to a car, they believe they have the strength and horsepower of their cars and will hurl insults at people twice their size. This seldom ends well.

The situation could be easily fixed if horns came with a simple regulator that you could adjust according to your mood. On a black dog day, you could set it to "extreme aggression" and it could emit an obnoxious shriek that annoyed everybody. Accompanying this with a shake of the arm could be a nice touch, particularly if you were convinced the person you were horning was not very big, or armed. It might also help if cars came with mechanical arms that made rude finger gestures to other drivers. This could significantly reduce repetitive strain injury among regular commuters and taxi drivers.

At the other end of the scale it could be set to "polite prompt" which would play a few notes of a Nora Jones song. This would make other drivers happy that you have acknowledged and warned them. They may even nod (the universal language of understanding between motorists all over the world).

The driver nod is evidence that not all humans turn feral behind the wheel. The close cousin of the driving nod is the courtesy wave. The courtesy wave is generally used by motorists to wave another motorist in front of them during a difficult merge, to acknowledge a polite gesture, or just to make a connection with an attractive fellow commuter. The courtesy wave has become such a strong force in driving protocol that other drivers now expect it. If someone lets you merge in and does not get a courtesy wave, this can make them very angry. This results in road rage and excessive use of the car horn.

Having so many human beings on the road at any one time requires countless volumes of rules so people don't run into each other or do dangerous things. There are so many rules that most people only know them for about an hour when they do a driving test as a teenager. For the rest of their driving life they rely on signs and gut instinct. As a result, people constantly run into each other and do dangerous things.

Even though motorists, when they are not actually in their cars, support road rules and road safety initiatives, once they are behind the wheel they regard these as a conspiracy by authorities to prevent them from moving quickly and getting the wind in their hair. Motorists generally believe that stopping them from speeding is designed purely to raise revenue for the greedy government. They regularly lament that police should be catching murderers rather than giving them tickets. This is despite deaths from car accidents in Australia outnumbering murders by hundreds to one.

While motorists generally hate other motorists and see them as the enemy of fast and efficient driving, when it comes to avoiding traffic authorities, they become united by a common enemy. As a result, drivers have developed a "secret" signal to tell other motorists when there is a police speed trap ahead. The secret signal is to flick their lights. Everyone, including the police, knows the secret signal so it is not a very good secret.

The light flick speed trap warning is probably the clearest sign we have that human beings do in fact care about their fellow travellers. There is really nothing in it for the motorists doing the flicking. In fact, they risk being arrested and charged with a heinous light-flicking crime. But they flick regardless, a gesture that says: "Fellow motorists, ahead is a speed camera that will cost you money. Slow down and go in peace."

Of course, the light flick also suggests that, despite the safety risks that come with speeding, motorists are more interested in stopping their fellow travellers from getting a ticket than in them adopting slower driving practices that might one day save their lives. Alternatively, their motives could be to slow people down, thus explaining why quite often you never come across a speed camera despite some mad flicking from the other side of the road.

In some places, you don't even need the light flash to tell you there is a camera ahead. There are certain fixed cameras that are in the same place all the time and the government puts up signs telling you they are ahead. Still, thousands of people get caught by these cameras every year. Perhaps in these cases the offence should be stupidity rather than speeding.

63. Space invaders

As well as having to deal with thousands of others on the roads, driving also requires us to find car parks where we can put our cars when they are not actually moving. The demand for car parks is generally about 30 per cent greater than the actual number of car parks. This makes the whole process like playing musical chairs. At any one time, dozens of cars can be circling in search of a spot.

As a result of this relative mathematical challenge, a busy shopping centre car park gives ordinary human drivers a scary glimpse into their primordial origins. The car park becomes important primitive hunting territory and a space must be fought for with guile, precision and very strong stares.

In the absence of any empty spaces, you must find people carrying shopping bags and follow them back to their car. When you think they are close, you put your indicator on. This is a traditional signal that you intend to take possession of the parking spot.

Sometimes, two or more vehicles will put their indicators on for the same car park. This becomes a battle of wits usually won by the person with the most frightening stare or the biggest bull bar.

Of course, once you have followed shoppers to a car parking space, they immediately go into slow motion, fussing over seat belts and adjusting trousers. This behaviour is hard to explain. They may just be total bastards. Or they may have worked so hard for the space, they are suffering separation anxiety.

As a pedestrian, one of the most stressful car park manoeuvres is the return-items-without-actually-leaving drop-off. In this instance, the dozens of cars that are waiting for a car space assume you are returning to your car to leave. When this does not happen they can become quite agitated. In these circumstances you must avoid eye contact and sudden movement. If you are particularly worried, run away and climb a tree. Upset drivers generally will not climb trees.

One of the other problems with trying to park your vehicle is that building developers do not really like car parks. They take up a lot of space, they are expensive to allocate and there is nothing architecturally pleasing about them. As a result, car parks around most buildings and apartments are seldom designed so actual cars can get into them. This is known as the developer car park revenge.

The most extreme examples of developer car park revenge can generally be found at coastal holiday units. These car parks are always built exactly too small to get a car in and out. As a result, regular coast unit renters have been forced to master the 34-point turn. This is a clever automotive exercise in which the car moves in, out, in, out, in, out, in, out, in, out, in, out (you are getting the idea) until it turns a 90deg angle using less than 2mm of clearance.

Coastal units are also like trees in the rainforest. They are all trying to break through the canopy so they can get a little glimpse of the sea. As a result, most units must be knocked down every few years to build a unit taller than the one across the road. This is a good thing because it allows recovery of all the cars that have become trapped in the garage after realising you can't do a 34-point turn in reverse.

Not content with impossible parking manoeuvres involving a single vehicle, humans decided to attach things to the back of vehicles to increase the driving and parking challenges. These are generally in the form of caravans or trailers.

Caravans are essentially homes on wheels. They tend to either be parked permanently at special caravan villages, because the owner could not be bothered moving them, or travel slowly along the national highways to a tourist destination.

Moving caravans are generally towed by older couples (known as grey nomads in some cultures) in large, early-model cars with giant side mirrors. They tend to travel about 30km/h below the actual speed limit and stand out because there is generally a line of traffic stretching back about 1km behind them trying to get past. Caravaners have been largely responsible for the boom in air transport as people work out that the only way to get past them is to fly over the top.

Grey nomads in caravans tend to stop every couple of hours to make cups of tea. During tea, they should only be approached by other grey nomads or people with time on their hands. A conversation started with a caravanning grey nomad during a tea break can last up to five hours and can cover everything from the poor state of other drivers, to politics and sport. Travelling grey nomad couples are generally so bored with each other's company they will seek out outside conversation with religious fervour. Sometimes they will even speak to wild animals. Over time, wild animals have become genetically tuned to areas frequented by grey nomads and will tend to avoid them.

At the end of the day, the nomads pull into a caravan park where they have to back their giant caravan into a tiny space next to a cement block. Generally the male driver does the backing and the female passenger yells the instructions and insults. The driver is generally fairly bad at backing the caravan and the passenger even worse at giving instructions. This can result in clothes lines and bins being demolished during the process. Caravan park proprietors expect this. They also know that many caravaners will drive off the next day with their vans still plugged into the electricity supply.

Backing trailers tends to be more of a mainstream pursuit because there are more trailers than caravans. In fact, backing a trailer is one of the last remaining tests of manhood, replacing early rituals like walking across hot coals and killing bears. Trailer-backing is particularly challenging because a reversing trailer does exactly the opposite of what the brain is expecting. This requires humans to override their brains, even though the brains are actually in charge and giving the directions. This seldom ends well.

Most trailer-backing tends to happen at the local rubbish dump, a strange communal haunt where humans unload their failures, broken dreams and excess tree branches. When you are a kid, the rubbish dump is about the most exciting place on earth. It's like a toy store where you don't have to worry about breaking anything. Kids, of course, cannot understand why adults throw all that great stuff away. They can always find 150 uses for an old mattress with no springs or a pram with only one wheel.

As you get older, the dump takes on a whole new significance. For men, it is the last bastion of male domination. You seldom see women at the dump. This is because, when it comes to equality, women draw the line at anything involving bad smells. Returning from a rubbish dump for modern men is akin to the cavemen returning from killing a mammoth. Women will give faint praise for the success of the mission and then proceed to sterilise your boots and burn the clothes you were wearing. Ideally they would insist on a two-day quarantine in the doghouse, but this would not be fair on the dog.

The garbage you take to the dump comes under unprecedented scrutiny in the new millennium. Back in the days when we weren't too worried about saving the planet, you just put everything in a big hole and a bulldozer came along and buried it. Now you must stop at least 47 times between the gate and the dumping point. Dumps have special sections for wood, oil, glass, paper, branches and life-sized headless statues of naked famous people, possibly Greeks. There are also now dump professionals who scrutinise your garbage for anything that might have any value. If the things you take to the dump are not in this category, the dump professionals look at you contemptuously. At this point you feel quite guilty and are tempted to say: "Sorry I know it's not much. I have some better stuff at home. I'll bring it next time." People feel under such pressure they end up taking all their good lounge furniture to the tip just to please the dump professionals.

Rubbish tips are essentially bloke places where you get rid of the bloke stuff like old bits of cement, rocks, tree branches and bits you took out of the car that don't seem to fit back anywhere. It is a place of male bonding where blokes flex their muscles and compete in unofficial tests of strength like hop, step and toss the old tyre, and hurl the piece of wood javelin contest. There is also the big rock shot put.

Of course, all of this pales into comparison against the ultimate trailer-backing test. Blokes pride themselves on their ability to back a trailer. If you can't back a trailer into a 2m wide spot, the other blokes look at you with contempt. It is like walking into a Wild West bar and ordering a sarsaparilla. This makes visiting the dump a high-pressure business.

Trailers were never actually designed for reversing. They are fine going straight ahead. They just cruise along and mind their own business, but as soon as you put the car into reverse they panic, sweat and move around like cornered worms. When your brain tells you to turn the wheel right, you must immediately override and turn the wheel left. If the trailer appears to be going straight you know it is teasing you and any minute it will move drastically and go sideways. Sometimes you are in a purple patch and you are able to complete the perfect trailer-back. This involves a single line-up, minimal steering wheel movement and landing the trailer in the middle of the target spot. The perfect tailer-back is rare, and when you pull it off it can leave you on a high for days. When it happens, you disembark from your car and look around with a humble, but slightly hoity, disposition. Other males at the dump will nod their approval. At this point you are king of the world.

Rubbish dumps are currently under threat because they are no longer considered politically correct. In future, it seems everything will be recycled, and secret underground societies of bloke-trailer-backers will have to be formed to satisfy male-bonding needs and compare trailer-backing superiority.

To some extent, dumps are already obsolete. A lot of people just put their rubbish in the trailer, don't bother covering it, and cruise to the dump at 150km/h. By the time they get there, nothing is left to unload. They are the ones you see at the dump sites scratching their heads and looking around saying: "Where'd it all go? Did you take it?" If these people were part of a different culture, you would put your money on the bears.

64. Looking like our cars

People with nothing better to occupy their time have observed that human animal-owners tend to look like their pets. This is sometimes true. If you look closely, it is also apparent that humans tend to look like their cars.

I have noticed this while sitting in peak-hour traffic with nothing better to do. Men driving large, well-polished sedans tend to wear a suit of the same colour, glasses the same shape as the headlights, and well-groomed hair. They wouldn't admit it, but they are probably the same people who, 20 years earlier, drove panel-vans with surfboards welded to the roof rack. The middle-age equivalent is a mobile phone glued to your ear.

Men in beat-up old green jeeps generally wear khaki shirts that would rust if they were any tougher, have an unshaven face, and look like they've taken a few bumps in their time. Young women in flashy sports cars with tinted windows always have long, streamlined hair and designer-tinted sunglasses. Men in big trucks are usually equally big and wear singlets.

Then there are those really luxurious four-wheel-drives. These cars are too expensive to get them dirty on an unsealed road, and you certainly wouldn't risk scratching the paint by going off-road. The drivers look a bit the same. They are usually in incredibly expensive designer "bush" gear that costs way too much to wear in the bush. For most of them, "roughing it" is staying at a motel with fewer than four stars. Sometimes they put the car into four-wheel drive to go up their steep driveway. This makes them feel like Indiana Jones.

The really interesting group are humans who drive Volkswagens covered in stickers. I'm having trouble describing them. I think they come from a different planet.

Drivers are at their most interesting when their cars break down. They immediately lift the bonnet and leave it open – an internationally recognised symbol that the car is a useless, good-for-nothing heap of crap and the owner is really pissed off about it. A dent in the side door caused by the driver kicking it is another such symbol.

In this situation, some people just sit there and wait for a mechanic to arrive. They know nothing about cars. There are people to do that sort of thing for them.

The people who are really fun to watch are the prodders. They know as little about cars as the first group, but are not prepared to admit it. Instead, they stick their head under the bonnet and start prodding. Then they crawl underneath and start prodding. I think they believe if they prod enough the car will suddenly burst into life. Unfortunately, to my knowledge (and I've been wrong before), no car has every burst back into life as a result of prodding.

This is the same group who, when the mechanic arrives and tells them their raspetutulator has come unstuck from the hugowatchacallit, say: "I thought that's what it was. That's what I would have looked at next."

The third group are the "just-enough" mechanics. They have the knowledge to rebuild their cars from scratch and, for this reason, they never maintain or fix anything. They drive around in bellowing, smoke-spitting, water-splattering, door-rattling, mind-numbing mechanical disasters. When the muffler falls off in the middle of the road, they whip out a piece of wire and put it back on. When the radiator springs a leak, they stop and fill it up every few minutes or try to plug it with some chewing gum. Eventually, they end up sitting in the middle of the highway holding just a steering wheel and thinking: "I really must fix that one day."

65. Don't park anywhere

One of the biggest problems with cars is that they are really good at getting you places, but once you get there you discover there's is no place to park them. Every year there are more cars and fewer car parks.

Eventually there will be no car parks at all. We will just take our cars out of the garage, drive around in circles and park back in the garage because that will be the only place we can legally leave them. This may require innovations like mid-trip mobile refueling and drive-through grocery stores.

Finding a parking spot in an urban area is one of the great human aspirations. This is because the parking spot equation almost never adds up. It is like a game of musical chairs. There are nearly always one or two fewer spaces at every venue compared with the number of cars looking for them. To succeed, you need to be quicker and smarter than the other drivers, and react with lightning speed when the music stops.

The best car parking spaces in any car park are the disabled spots. These are nearly always empty, but most people are okay with this because it suggests a relatively low rate of disability in the community. They like the fact that should a disabled person ever show up at the shopping centre, they will indeed have somewhere to park.

Most drivers will try to cram their cars into an impossibly small space before they will walk more than 100m from the vehicle to a venue. Most humans will consider it their birthright to have a close car park and will go to any length to redeem it.

Getting a car into a small parking space generally requires a manoeuvre called the reverse park. The reverse park is generally perfected by teenagers when they first get their licence and then avoided for all the driving years that follow. This is because it is really easy to misjudge the manoeuvre and have to repeat it. While you are doing this, traffic is generally building up behind you and other drivers are casting aspersions on your upbringing. Most drivers have three goes at the reverse park and then speed off in embarrassment and frustration. Most times they can find another easier-to-access spot 100m away and just walk to the venue.

66. Flying high

My children often tell me that the only piece of wisdom I have ever given them is this: "Two wrongs don't make a right, but two Wrights made an aeroplane." This, of course, refers to the Wright brothers, credited as the pioneers of modern flight.

Once humans realised that cars were not going to get them everywhere they needed to go, and that they might spend a significant proportion of their lives waiting for caravans to stop for morning tea, they turned their attention to the skies. The sky is a good place to travel. There is a lot of it, only a limited number of people can use it and, once you get high enough, there is not a lot in the way.

Humans have something of a morbid fascination with flight. Deep down most of them are actually terrified of it. They know it is not actually possible for a plane to be in the air. It is way too heavy and only stays there because we keep it moving forward at an incredible speed before gravity and physics are able to do their thing. As a result, as comedian Tommy Cooper pointed out, if you go to a public library and scream at the top of your voice everyone will tell you to be quiet. But if you do the same thing in a plane, everyone joins in.

Air travel is, in fact, very safe. The whole industry is built around safety. I read once that, based on the odds, if you flew in a plane every day, you could fly for an average of 21,000 years before you would be in a crash.

The trouble is, we are always being reminded about the possibility of something going wrong. Any aircraft problem anywhere in the world is a big story. Hundreds of movies have been made about things going wrong on planes, everything from letting snakes loose, to amateurs having to land the plane when the pilot takes ill from the in-flight chicken.

We are also reminded every single time we fly about what we need to do in an emergency. There are oxygen masks dropping out of the ceiling, life jackets under the seat, seat belts that must be fastened while we are seated in case the plane drops suddenly, and rafts that the crew will operate in an emergency. If you sit in the economy seats with the extra leg room, you must be prepared to open the emergency door if things go wrong. This puts you under a fair bit of pressure, but at least you know you are in a good spot to get out.

For anyone who doesn't fly a lot, it must seem like these types of emergencies are fairly routine. Everyone is so blasé about the briefings that it would be easy to believe that the crew was constantly breaking out the rafts or that there was a regular need for oxygen and getting our own mask working before helping others.

Modern air travel, however, is mostly about the food. A modern airport is really just a big restaurant with planes. When you are in the air, the flight revolves around the in-flight service. If you fly at the right time, you get an actual meal. There is great anticipation about the meal. The pilot will implore us to enjoy the in-flight service. The head steward will assure us that the in-flight service will commence shortly.

Food is also an important part of the in-flight class system. Even though everyone is on the same plane, airlines realised long ago that in-flight society needed to be divided into socio-economic segments. First class and business class are always at the front of the plane. This means that the economy class people have to walk through this area to get to the small seats with no leg room at the back. This is designed to show them how the rest of the world lives and rub their noses in their relative lack of success. During the flight, the economy cabin is often separated from the front cabins by a curtain. This is apparently to stop any fraternisation between the economy and first class passengers. There might also be better air in the front.

Airline staff are trained to greet business and first-class passengers slightly friendlier than the other passengers. They often call you by name and give you a special smile. Before you take off, they give you juice. And immediately after take-off, you get a hot towel. This adds about $400 to the cost of the flight. It is very good juice.

In the film *Jerry Maguire*, the character Dorothy (played by Renee Zellweger) observes that first class used to be a better meal, but now it is a better life. But it still is a better meal. In fact, the big difference between economy and the other classes is choice. In economy you often just get the one meal, unless you have special dietary requirements and give lots of notice. The meal comes in a square plastic container with an aluminium lid. You don't really know what you are getting until the lid comes off. This delays the disappointment.

In business and first class, you generally get a choice of two meals (provided you are not the last person served). Your special steward or stewardess announces your choices with the precise detail of a restaurant maître d'. They will often use a slightly European accent and there is the promise of extra bread and unlimited alcohol. If the flight is long enough, you may get a refill on your coffee. Meals are produced from a magic cart on wheels that seems to contain a lot more food than could possibly be in there.

The role of airline steward or stewardess is considered quite glamorous. It is not really clear why. These people spend most of their working day in confined spaces, serving packaged food from a little cart. They spend much of their lives living in hotels out of little suitcases and getting up at strange hours to fly to places they do not necessarily want to go. All day they are forced to smile at people they do not necessarily like. Almost every flight is the same, and sometimes they fly through storms and turbulence that throw them all over the sky. Yep, you can see why that's a glamorous job.

The biggest leap of faith when humans fly is believing that their luggage will end up at the same destination as them. This represents the ultimate in wishful thinking.

When you check in for your flight, you entrust your luggage to a conveyor belt in the fervent hope that, despite dozens of planes leaving for all over the world every few minutes, your suitcase will end up on the right one. The system relies on the efficiency of people who drive around the airport in little carts that would be equally at home as the $1-a-ride novelty train at the local fete. The luggage is then tossed around like rugby balls and lumped into the cargo area with dozens of identical bags.

Every flight seems to have someone with odd-shaped luggage like a wind surfer or a totem pole. These are usually carried on by groups of people in matching T-shirts representing sports that you have never heard of.

When you arrive at your destination, you go quickly to the baggage conveyor belt so you know whether your luggage has arrived or if you are destined to wear the same socks and underwear for the next four days. After about 10 minutes, the conveyor beast stirs into life. There are always about six bags on the belt that come out in the first batch. Nobody ever claims these. This is because the bags are apparently empty and put on the conveyor belt by the airline to give passengers confidence that their bag might be coming.

Nothing is sadder than a person watching the empty conveyor for 10 minutes in the forlorn hope that their bag will arrive. Equally sad is a stray bag going round and round with no one claiming it. These are known as suitcase orphans. Generally, airline welfare workers eventually find good homes for them. Unclaimed totem poles are seldom so lucky.

67. Aircraft lounges

After air travel became popular, airlines had to find a way to keep passengers occupied as they waited for hours between flights. At first they just put seats in the gate lounges and installed a few televisions. Eventually, however, wealthy travellers tired of the seats and the television and started demanding their own space to wait for their flights. This led to the birth of the airport lounge.

The airport lounge is an exclusive area with seats and televisions but hidden away from normal passengers in a secret part of the airport. Regular travellers pay hundreds of dollars to access the lounge, which also has free drinks and soup. Over time, more and more people have found ways to join the lounge and now it is mostly loud and chockers. Smart people now go back to the seats and television at the departure gate, which is free and mostly quiet.

Keeping up appearances

68. Dress code

After someone went to a lot of trouble to design the human body and make it a thing of beauty, our brains decided at some point in the past that parts of it really needed to be covered up. This was a very good thing for the fashion industry, which could never have reached its current status in a totally nude world.

Of course, when our cave person ancestors first donned skins and fur to keep warm and protect vital parts from saber-toothed cats, they would not have known the misery, hours of indecision, wardrobe malfunctions and social status issues that would arise as a consequence. They also could not have foreseen the future backlash against wearing fur.

Choosing clothing is probably the most stressful decision we ever make in life. Everyone wants to be noticed but not to stand out. We want to be individual but also in fashion. Part of the problem with clothes is that the rules on what you should wear are fairly hazy. In some industries this problem has been resolved by wearing uniforms. In most cases, however, the fashion "rules" are couched in vague concepts like business attire, smart casual, semi-formal, formal, cocktail, evening wear, day suit, lounge suit, black tie, white tie, fancy dress and, my personal favourite, "evening casual".

The problem with these fashion rules is that there are very broad interpretations of what people mean by them. The rules also change every few years and nobody tells you until you arrive at a board lunch wearing a Daffy Duck tie with flashing lights on it.

In my home state of Queensland, Australia, there was a time when the difference between casual and formal came down to the thickness of the strap on your thongs (as in the footwear, known a flip-flops in some cultures). Now casual can mean any type of clothes you feel comfortable wearing, and formal usually involves some sort of suit for men (ties apparently optional) and for women something that costs at least $250 and has a "designer" label. Nobody is ever really sure what a designer label is, especially given that all clothes must at some point have had a designer, but it helps if the label sounds Italian or French and the "Made in China" tag is well hidden.

Black tie once meant your suit had to be black with flap things on the back and you had to wear a fluffy three musketeers shirt and a bowtie that made you look like a hog-tied magpie. Now some people don't wear ties at all (black tie with no tie!). Any dark suit seems to pass. In fact, the really cool people just wear an open shirt, sometimes with chest hair showing. The slightly eccentric wear a bright-coloured suit, particularly yellow or purple (black tie with no black!). Hopefully this trend will pass soon. Nothing good every came from a yellow suit.

Smart casual is another mystery. Presumably it is the opposite to dumb-arse casual and requires you to have a clean shirt and at least joggers on your feet. It once would have required that you tuck in your shirt. But no-one tucks their shirts in any more. Except older men. Older men tuck in everything. In fact, every fashion rule goes out the window when it comes to older men. Comedian Jerry Seinfeld astutely observed that older men seem to find a fashion era and never move out of it for the rest of their lives. Older men like "comfortable" shorts – not too long, not too short – with substantial manly material and pockets for easy storage. Their shirts are plain and functional. On occasions they lash out and buy a checked shirt (for barn dances) or, during a mid-life crisis, a Hawaiian shirt that gets worn once and spends the rest of its wretched life hanging in the back of the cupboard.

Despite the different terms used in event invitations, there appears to be no scientific difference between a lounge suit and other types of suits. Same with a dress suit. That apparently covers any suit that you get dressed in. It may disqualify casual suits even though suits, by definition, are not meant to be casual. As for the day suit, who knows? Is this a suit you wear during the day and not at night? And if so, what is the difference? The only thing everyone agrees on is that a Safari Suit, created during a short-lived brain explosion during the 1970s, should never be worn in public. Or in private.

Much of our fashion sense and enduring beliefs about clothing psychology stem from our childhood. My mother always insisted that I not wear the same good shirt to Sunday school two weeks in a row. "People will think you only have one shirt," she rationalised. And she was probably right. In fact, I'm sure the whole thing had the makings of a fairly serious one-shirt scandal that would have brought shame on my family and friends over a number of generations. You can just imagine it. The Jones family get home from church and start saying things like: "Did you notice Rodgers wore the same shirt this week as last week?" "I did," another of the Joneses would say. "I wonder if he only has one shirt," another would muse. Such a thing would allow the Joneses with their multiple shirt cupboards to sit around smugly and develop a superior fashion attitude and a hoity gait.

Such problems do not end with childhood. Throughout their lives people work hard at creating an illusion that they have a wardrobe of Imelda Marcos dimensions. There is some form of unwritten code that dictates respectable distances between the wearing of the same outfit to work or formal occasion. This is based on an assumption that someone, besides yourself, is actually keeping tabs; which is highly unlikely. Most men in a workplace situation have a distinct advantage in this regard because they have a staple clothes diet of suit, shirt and tie. Suits all look so much alike that you can wear the same one every couple of days and avoid any serious breach of the code.

Business shirts too. The only real difference between a $30 white shirt and an $80 one is $50 and the name of some French guy that you can't pronounce. (This has changed somewhat lately as men move towards shirts in darker shades of blue, green and stripes. In this pursuit there is a fine line between being trendy and looking like one of the Wiggles). Ties are a bit trickier. In fact, the whole male work dress concept revolves around the tie diversion. Change the tie every day and no-one will notice the rest. There are varying opinions on the safe distance between wearing the same tie. I think it is somewhere between four and 10 days.

Of course, there are many other factors which can have a serious impact on clothing dynamics. The clothing taint, for example. Some years ago a colleague asked if the blue shirt I was wearing was part of my old school uniform. I looked down at the shirt. The shirt looked up at me. We both knew this was the end. The shirt was tainted. The taint is death for clothing. Sure the shirt will still be ironed and hung back in the closet, but it can never resume its place among the normal daily clothes options. At best it will be worn to paint a chair or do the mowing. More likely it will be quietly slipped into a charity bin and taken off for a new life. The charity bin is the clothing equivalent of the witness protection program.

Sometimes, on quiet, balmy summer nights you sit and reflect on what became of the shirts you gave away. Did they find good homes? Are they being treated well? Is the new owner using the fabric softener and only washing them with similarly-coloured clothes. Perhaps, sometime in the future, governments will set up programs that help people reunite with their shirts. This will be fairly emotional and may call for a special reality television program.

In another instance some years earlier, a colleague suggested a shirt I was wearing looked like a pyjama top. I looked down at the shirt. The shirt looked up at me. We both knew I had dressed in the dark and this *was* my pyjama top. Just kidding. It was really a gift from my wife. This made it safe. Spousal gifts are immune from taint. You just have to wear them and accept the consequences. If anyone says anything, all you have to say is "gift from the wife" (or girlfriend or mother for that matter) and people will give a knowing and fairly sympathetic nod and just leave you alone. In fact, once you are seriously partnered in life, the choice of what to wear is taken out of your hands. All clothing decisions become subject to spousal veto, usually exercised with the dreaded question: "You're not wearing that are you?". "Ahhhh, I guess not", is the conventional reply.

Of course, men do not have the same option when it comes to fashion veto. The only role of the male in helping women to choose what to wear is to agree with everything and insist that nothing makes their bum look big. In fact, you should never mention the bum in the same sentence as clothing. The two subjects require a strict church and state separation.

From about the age of 14, women develop an affliction called Exaggerated Audience Syndrome. This basically means they believe that whenever they are out in public everyone is looking at them and generally making an assessment about what they are wearing. They suffer this syndrome because it is usually true. Women are obsessed with what other people are wearing. They spend hours looking at magazines full of people wearing things. Women can talk for hours about what people are wearing. This is considered acceptable human female dialogue unless people are talking about them. In that case, it is known as bitchiness.

Often fashion trends are dictated by celebrities and pop culture "fashion leaders". This happens because people believe if they dress like cool people, they will also be cool. This is largely delusional. It also means celebrities have to keep changing their styles to avoid being dressed like all the geeks who have copied their trends. When Brian Epstein convinced The Beatles to wear suits and hairstyles that looked like mops, he set a new standard in what rocks stars should wear on stage. Unfortunately, the standard was fairly low and performers have avoided suits and mop-tops ever since.

Despite this, over the years many performers have used clothes to make a statement. Johnny Cash wore black to convey a certain blackness, Elvis wore jump-suit things to save him changing out of his pyjamas, the Beach Boys wore floral shirts for obvious reasons (sheer elegance) and Kiss wore clothes so ugly they had been discarded even by the Mardi Gras. The Bay City Rollers caused an outbreak of tartan (albeit briefly), ABBA tried everything from velvet to cocktail dresses, and Split Enz had some sort of Addams Family thing going that didn't really catch on. Michael Jackson for some years dressed like a science-fiction alien commander, and Billy Idol looked like he had been subjected to a particularly nasty bachelor party trick.

Alas, today some of the subtle art of rock star fashion statement has been lost. Now, even though they are earning millions, most stars look like they have struggled to find an ironed shirt in the drawer and the one they chose was probably purchased from the retro section of a charity disposal store. The one possible exception is Marilyn Manson, who has managed to have a successful musical career without ever having been a Mouseketeer. Manson makes a fashion statement every time he goes out in public. That statement is something like: "Arrgghhhhhhhhgh".

Madonna also made cowboy hats cool again when she released an album wearing an actual hat. Avril Lavigne had girls wearing ties around their necks, and Eminem prompted thousands of people to wear beanies in the middle of summer. Britney Spears, inspired by a generation of plumbers with low-hanging, butt-revealing King Gee work shorts, started wearing clothes that rose up and sat down – leaving the stomach area exposed. Within months there was a sea of stomachs as far as the eye could see. Britney is now wearing progressively less clothing, making people nervous about calling a plumber.

Sporting stars can also start fashion trends, even though most of them seem to have an innate hatred of shirts. In times of extreme emotion, elite sportspeople rip their shirts off as if to say: "Now I am important I no longer have to put up with this shirt." Shirt hatred is particularly pronounced in soccer (football) where players routinely pull off their shirts after scoring a goal. US women's soccer team player Brandi Chastain caused a sensation when she pulled off her top after scoring the winning goal in the World Cup in 1999. Sometimes soccer players just pull the shirts over their heads, causing them to flail around like a dying bug. This is always funny until someone runs into a pole (a pylon, not a Polish person).

Tennis players have also been known to do the shirt thing. Thousands flocked to Anna Kournikova tennis matches for years just in case she ever won and ripped off her shirt. Didn't happen.

Shirt hatred dates back to the early caveman days when hunters would remove their bear skins after a good clubbing. In Roman times, the gladiators would pull off their armour and scream. Sometimes this was because they had won. Other times it was because they had a bloody great sword jammed into their buttocks. In modern times, shirt removal has become so rife that international football codes have considered making it a "cautionable offence", which sounds very bad but may be necessary to protect harmless clothing from fashion abuse.

Fashion trends can also have their origins in practical pursuits. The newest must-have fashion accessory for the Australian male is the glow-in-the-dark vest. As infrastructure becomes the new black and construction workers proliferate, all males are trying to outdo themselves to stand out from the crowd during the day and light up like Las Vegas neon when they man the stop-go sign at night. The trend is now being taken up by political leaders trying to look macho, and it is only a matter of time before it infiltrates the business office, school grounds and movie wardrobe departments.

In a sense, the fluoro vest is a return to primordial mating rituals, generally practised by birds and insects, in which the male must prove himself to be the biggest and the brightest to attract a mate. As a result, construction sites will soon replace the internet as the mating ground of choice, and the fluoro vests will become louder, brighter and heavily immersed in Lynx. The trend will be useful in Christmas lights season. Instead of wasting time with trees, we can just decorate a few construction workers.

The ultimate clothing relationship occurs between humans and their shoes. Men tend to have a comfortable, workmanlike relationship with their shoes. Male shoes are a bit like a dog – reliable, respectful and always there when you need them. The male shoe never questions the terrain. It takes whatever comes along. The male shoe is proud and strong. And the relationship is monogamous.

The female shoe relationship is very different. Women and their shoes have a fickle relationship. Women cannot just have one or two pairs of shoes. They must have more. Dozens are not enough. A woman can never have enough shoes. While men never notice what shoes other people are wearing, it is the first thing women notice. To men, most women's shoes look pretty much the same. Women can spot subtle differences from 11 metres away. Men like comfortable shoes. Women will balance on 10cm heels and squeeze each foot into an area half of its mass if they think the shoe looks good.

Buying a pair of shoes is much the same as dating. It begins when you see the shoe on the rack. Something about it catches your eye and you move in to make the first tentative contact. If the shoe looks just as good close up, you carefully slip it on. At first it feels a bit tight and strange as you move your toes and look for signs of compatibility with your foot.

If this goes well, it is time for the first "date" – the walk around. You slowly walk around the store wondering if these might indeed be the shoes for you. At this stage your head is full of questions: Will they give me support when I need it most? Will they still look this good in six months? Will they adapt and mould to my feet or stay rigid and take their own path? Will they still need me when I'm 64? If the answers are favourable, it is time to move in together and begin the challenges of daily life.

For a while the shoes are out every night dancing and carefree. But inevitably the passion dies and they languish in the cupboard and the relationship becomes familiar, comfortable and practical. The good shoe relationships can last many years. But many end after just a few years and there is a parting of ways at the charity bin in the supermarket car park.

Sometimes when you first see the shoe, it is love at first sight. You grab it, try it on, buy it and bolt from the store. This usually ends badly. By the time you get home you realise the shoe doesn't fit and you either walk around in misery for a while or quickly discard it. This is the dreaded one-wear stand.

69. Reflected glory

Human beings tend to have a love-hate relationship with mirrors. On the downside, mirrors are a two-dimensional reminder that we are getting old, having a bad hair day or we have put on 10kg. On the upside, a mirror in a dark area can take years off your face and remove the blemishes associated with attacks by nature and gravity.

Many humans are so drawn to a mirror they cannot walk past one without looking at their reflection. This is particularly the case in shopping centres where there are mirrors all over the place that prompt people to adjust their hair or check their waistline in silhouette. Mostly we are looking for a mirror miracle – some evidence that we look better than we thought or we have developed six-pack stomachs and high cheek bones without exercise or surgery.

Our lives are full of good and bad mirror experiences. Generally, any mirror that looks up at us will give us multiple chins. Mirrors in strong sunlight will make us look washed out and mottled. Mirrors on ceilings mostly freak us out, and full-length mirrors give us too much information.

Some people cannot even resist a mirror when driving. Each morning many female motorists apply make-up and make hair adjustments looking into the rear view mirror.

This is achieved with the car travelling at 80km/h, during thunderstorms, with cars darting in and out in front of them and with no hand apparently on the steering wheel.

Perhaps the most-feared mirror is the one in a shop changing room. In this case, one whole wall of the tiniest room ever built contains your reflection. There is nowhere to hide. This is where all humans must take stock of how they really look. This can be quite traumatic.

The experience is particularly disturbing because it also highlights the difference between the way you see yourself and how you really are. When you pick up the piece of clothing off the rack, you imagine it will look as good on you as it does on the mannequin with no head. Generally, however, it is two sizes too small and makes you look bloated.

A similar phenomenon exists with tape recorders and photographs. Only the very vain generally think they look good in photographs. In fact, humans have such a strong sense of self image that only rarely will they find a photo that matches their own perception. Such a photograph will be used over and over. Older people, in particular, often avoid being photographed at all. In their mind, they are still 20 but this is no longer reflected in the visual evidence. There is a great line in the John Denver song *Some Days are Diamonds*: "Now the face that I see in my mirror, more and more is a stranger is to me."

Even celebrities become very picky about photographs of themselves and how they are used. Some insist on being photographed through filtered lenses. Curiously, most other people can barely tell the difference between a good picture and a bad picture of someone else. This is because people can never really know what they look like in 3-D and rely heavily on mirrors and photographs for a visual guide. The only exception to this would be identical twins. I assume this would provide a great opportunity to have your twin try on clothes for you so you can see if your bum really does look big.

The voice is even more intriguing. When Australians watch an American television program, the actors do not seem to have accents. Yet, when the actors visit as themselves for promotions, the accent sounds rich, broad and foreign.

Almost everyone thinks their own voice sounds "funny" when it is recorded. This is because the way the human ear hears its person's own voice is slightly different from the way the rest of the world hears it. When we hear ourselves speak, the sound comes to us through our jaws and our heads. When we hear it externally, it just goes through the air. Logically, this means our recorded voice is the most accurate. This explains why some people should never sing.

Even famous singers often say they prefer to perform live because they believe recordings distort their voices. This is less the case for children, who seem to love tape recorders. Mostly they just scream into them. Children seem to be constantly amazed that they are able to scream. They are particularly happy that they can record a scream and play it back. They seldom complain that the scream sounds funny.

70. Hats

Even though humans have been living on the planet for many thousands of years, they can't actually go outside without getting fried by the sun. To overcome this, science has invented hats. Hats sit on heads and repel the sun. They are also an important fashion accessory.

Some people, particularly cowboys, can wear a hat all the time and it just looks like an extension of their heads. Others never look right wearing hats and prefer to just fry in the sun and live with the consequences (which are usually cancer and death). They logic that looking bad in a hat is actually worse than death.

For some people, the fear of the hat is almost as bad as the fear of hat hair. Hat hair is a chronic hair affliction caused by wearing hats for excessive periods. It results in the hair being forced unnaturally against the head and sitting there like a bundled hay bail until it gets a shock shampoo treatment. Ordinary hair implements like combs and brushes are virtually useless in the face of hat hair. It is one of nature's most powerful forces.

The human obsession with hats begins in childhood when parents constantly nag their children about wearing a hat outside. Every child owns approximately four hats and a roughly equal number is missing at any one time. To counter this, parents also have spare hats. These are hats previously owned by older siblings or given away as promotions by well-meaning corporations. Spare hats never fit properly and nearly always look like they have had a very hard life. Sometimes, a spare hat can survive 40 years and two generations without succumbing to cloth disintegration. This long life is generally attributed to neglect and having never being washed.

The most prestigious hats are worn by women at race meets. No outfit can generally win a "fashions in the field" prize without a great hat. These often come with a feather. It is not clear why they come with a feather or the status of the original feather owner. It is clear that a good feather can make a huge difference to quality of a race course outfit. Increasingly, horse racing is less about betting and more about standing around in hats. Few humans can explain why this is so. It might have something to do with cheap alcohol.

The most basic form of hat is called a cap. It consists of a dome to cover your head and a single protruding brim that looks like a duck bill. The duck bill is designed to shade your face from the sun. Necks and ears just have to take their chances. During the

1990s, young people started to wear their caps backwards. This seemed to be based on a collective realisation that the neck was important too. After a few years of this, somebody noticed that the face was now totally unprotected. This caused a collective realisation that the face was important too and everyone except a couple of tennis players returned the cap to the default position. This prompted the advice from humourist Dan Zevin that you should never wear a backward cap to a job interview unless the job is "umpire".

71. Hair today

If our eyes are the window on our souls, our hair must be the antenna of our moods. No matter what we say with our mouths, our hair gives away how we are really doing. After a late night, people will ask how you are feeling. "Fine," you say. But your hair tells a different story. If it is frazzled and out of whack, people look at it knowingly and think "hangover". In fact, no matter how much fusion-fracted, herbal-enforced hair product you attack it with, your hair always tells the truth. You might fight ageing, but your hair goes grey anyway. You may pretend you are not scared on the roller-coaster, but your hair gives you away by freaking out and standing on end.

I think hair-honesty exists because the hair has such a strategic position on the body, linking directly into the brain. Based on this theory, each hair is really a tiny antenna picking up our emotional signals. Scientists have known this for some time and have devoted much time and energy to devising ways to suppress the hair's natural emotional instincts. Hairdressers use giant hair torture chambers that women sit under for hours with aluminium foil in their hair. This is a form of hair nuking that seeks to break the emotional link between the hair and the brain. This seldom works. Hair, through centuries of genetic evolution, is generally more than a match for foil and nuclear fusion.

Another major assault in the war on hair emotion was the

invention of Brylcream. In the 1960s and 1970s guys wore it by the bucket-load. Brylcream destroyed any hint of emotion in your hair. If you caked on enough of it, no hair moved for days, sometimes weeks. Once it set, your head became like a force-field capable of repelling sunlight, wildlife and attractive women.

Hair, along with fingernails, represents the body's renegade external elements. When the brain sends out the message to other parts of the body to stop growing, the hair and fingernails just keep going. As a result of this hair delinquency, mankind, as if it didn't have enough to worry about, must contend with hairstyles.

For most of my childhood, the hairstyle came via the home-haircut kit. There was a sense of foreboding in the house on home-haircut day. Even Brylcream struggled to stop hair panicking itself into an unnatural perm. (Speaking of perms, this was also, of course, the heyday of the famous home perm – another attempt by scientists to beat hair into submission. Ordinary women with ordinary hair could take an ordinary-looking bottle and come out looking like a cross between Shirley Temple and Weird Al Yankovic. For years, this was considered a good thing. Today, few people talk about it, preferring to forget the whole sorry business. As a result, most photographs from the 1980s have been quietly destroyed).

In truth, my mother was highly skilled with the home-haircut kit. Besides, it was a choice of that or the barber. Boys feared the barber. He had only two cuts in his repertoire – short and very short. The boys who had "very short" came out resembling startled porcupines. The boys who chose short also came out looking like startled porcupines. On reflection, I think the barber actually had only one cut in his repertoire.

Eventually, it became acceptable for blokes to have their hair done at a hairdresser. This was far more civilised because they gave you books full of pictures of really cool hairstyles. You just picked one out and they gave it to you. Unfortunately, cool hairstyles only seem to last about an hour. Wash it, or stand in the wind, and they always seem to revert back to the same one you've had since you were 10.

Of course, the big gun in the battle between man and hair has long been that most cherished of Australian icons – the hair curler. The plastic hair curler is a small plastic device that can be inserted into hair to contort it into a curl. It is a portable torture device for hair and was a product of less-enlightened times, and before President Obama banned torture. In the 1950s and 1960s, no Australian housewife would be caught dead talking at the fence without a particularly ugly pink dressing gown and plastic hair curlers wrapped in a scarf. It was generally believed that the best way to convince hair to mend its delinquent ways was to lock it up in curlers for long periods.

Today, women have mostly abandoned the idea of curling their hair and have reverted to the equally tortuous hair straightener to remove any natural curls that may have invaded their generics. This is generally considered bad for the bread industry. As children, we were told if we ate the crusts of our bread, then our hair would curl. Nowadays, that is the last thing anybody would want to happen. I fear the new millennium may be a bad one for crusts.

In modern terms, there is also greater interest in rehabilitating hair in the hope that it will take a useful place in society and eventually conform to acceptable standards of bodily behaviour. But there is still a certain right-wing element which rejects this approach to hair discipline as too soft and wants to bring back the plastic hair curlers. They argue, with some statistical backing, that since the waning of Brylcream and hair curlers, there has been a startling increase in bad hair days, helmet hair and artificial afros. Others blame it on foreigners and a gradual breakdown in hair values. While in the past parents disciplined their children's hair and were always home to plough it with a big brush, now it is too often left to the care of others, or allowed to grow wild.

72. Male pyjamas

There is something particularly tragic about men's pyjamas. Despite years of trying to find appropriate attire for men to wear to bed, whatever we use seems totally out of sync with the human body and ill-suited to the task.

In winter, many men wear long flannelette pyjamas tied at the waist with a rope. These pyjamas seem to exist purely to use up flannelette. Flannelette is a mysterious fabric used only at night or by lumberjacks. It is almost impossible to look cool in flannelette. It can only be worn at home after dark, or in the middle of the forest.

The big problem with long flannelette pyjamas is keeping them up. If you pull the rope tight enough to hold them up, it cuts off all circulation to your lower body. If you leave the rope loose, the pants fall to your knees every time you stand up. The other problem is synchronising the movement of your body with the movement of the flannelette pyjamas. There is generally so much fabric in these pyjamas that when you roll one way, the pyjamas are still facing the other. You and your pyjamas spend all night trying to catch up with each other. By morning, you are exhausted and somewhat knotted.

Jerry Seinfeld has observed that men are so obsessed with suits, their pyjamas have been made like little suits – collars, buttons, pockets, the works. Next thing we know, men will have little night-time ties and jackets. These will almost certainly need dry cleaning.

In summer, with some relief, men retire the flannelette pyjamas and break out the "shorty" pyjamas. The shorties are a matching shirt and pants that make you feel like you are about to partake in martial arts. Being seen in shorty pyjamas is the most embarrassing thing that can happen to a man. A man would rather be caught naked or in a chicken suit than in his shorty pyjamas. Sometimes these pyjamas come in spots and stripes. It is important to change out of these on Christmas morning. Otherwise you may end up photographed and immortalised. This picture would inevitably be brought out if you ever became Prime Minister or President.

In more recent times, younger men have abandoned the shorty pyjamas in favour of T-shirts and shiny boxer shorts. This is an equally unattractive combination, particularly as the shiny boxers are usually adorned with pictures of cars, bananas, super heroes or cartoon characters. Like most pyjamas, these are nearly always a size too big.

Of course, the only thing worse than the pyjamas men wear at home are the ones they get in the hospital. These versions are like giant baby bibs and are generally 10cm too short to cover everything. This means that when you are in hospital, instead of just walking, all the patients have two hands behind their backs and do a sort of squat, waddle, dance to get around. You can spot the difference between the medical staff and the patients: The staff walk down the middle of the hallways, while the patients slink along the walls trying desperately to avoid exposing their bums.

Of course, wearing nice pyjamas at home is very important because, as all parents tell their children, your house might burn down – and you don't want to be stuck outside in stripy flannelette pants fallen to your knees when the television crews arrive. Why do parents worry about things like that? It's like when they tell you to wear clean underwear in case you have a car accident. What do they think is going to happen? As they wheel you into the emergency room, the doctor says: "Get this patient ready for surgery. Oh, hang on. Can't do it. Bad underpants."

Family life

73. Mating

In order to ensure the survival of the human race, it is important for male and female humans to mate. Despite this, nature designed men and women so they have approximately nothing in common and mostly don't get on very well. Even so, men and women spend a considerable amount of their time trying to attract members of the opposite sex.

Women seek attention by dressing well, looking after their appearance and acting like they are not interested in men. Men attract attention by drinking too much, driving their cars too fast and using pick-up lines like: "Hey baby, fancy a spin?" Male pick-up lines pretty much never work, but men have been persevering with them for centuries, refusing to admit the idea has no merit. It is not clear how men and women ever actually form partnerships and breed. Generally this is put down to alcohol and desperation.

Nature is pretty much over pick-up lines and has been quietly conspiring to get rid of men completely so women no longer need to endure them. Now that equality is well established, the only remaining use for men appears to be to produce sperm. However, scientists recently announced that they had managed to produce sperm in a laboratory. It now seems only a matter of time before we will have an all-female world. This will result in a vastly changed social environment. The world will be dominated by long silences, shoes and older Matthew McConaughey movies with predictable endings. Chuck Norris may no longer be considered the ultimate role model for young people. Until then, however, there will be multi-gender families...

74. Birth

If you believe in evolution, you probably accept it is only a matter of time before children are born with remote controls. This would make parenting a lot easier. When the children cried loudly you could just turn the volume down a bit. When you wanted them to tidy their rooms a bit quicker, you'd hit fast-forward. And when they did something cute, you could just rewind them and see it again. If you had to nip out of the room, you could hit the pause button and know your child was safe until you returned. If you wanted them to sleep, you could just cut the power.

These are the types of things you have a lot of time to think about when you are walking around your house in the small hours of the morning with a new-born that has yet to discover the nuances of night and day.

Birth tends to be a wonderful experience for men. For woman it looks more like Chinese bamboo torture. All of our children were delivered via a procedure called a caesarean or "caesar", which I assume was named after the famous Roman emperor who also got the knife. Some people call this birth "the easy way". If this is easy, I thank my lucky stars I was born male.

Mind you, it probably is the easy way for men. Instead of sitting around for hours being abused by your wife while you say intelligent things like "breathe" and "don't push yet" in a conventional labour, it is all over in less than an hour. The downside is, before they will let you in for the birth, you must wear a particularly unsightly shower cap and footwear borrowed from Santa's elf helpers.

Before the operation, I had two key responsibilities. While my wife was being wheeled from the ward to the operating theatre, I had to push the lift button. Unfortunately, I hit the wrong one and the whole operating party ended up face-to-face with a crowd of bemused visitors on the ground floor.

My other role was custodian of the all-important camera so we could capture the birth for perpetuity. Unfortunately, posterity will have to put up with one photo because I forgot to put the new film in. No-one made much of a fuss of this because men have never been much good when it comes to birth. They are supposed to act like hopeless clods. That's our job.

In ages past, the men used to sit outside chain-smoking until the baby was born. Back then, birth was a hazardous business for fathers. If the stress didn't kill them, the cigarettes would. Now they figure it is safer to have them on the inside so if they pass out or hyperventilate, there are lots of medical people around to give them a shot of something or some gas. Even so, hospital authorities are still coming to grips with what the father is supposed to do at the birth. Just before the operation they leave him on public display alone on a round stool in the middle of the warm-up room. There is a limit to how intelligent you can look sitting there in your shower cap and elf boots.

When you finally get your call, the doctor informs you that you are in charge of the wellbeing of the top of your wife's head during the procedure. I realised fairly quickly this was not as important as it sounded. There was not an awful lot to do up there. It was clear the real action was further down.

That aside, the birth itself is one of those really magical experiences. One minute you are sitting there applying your extensive medical knowledge to the top of your wife's head and the next you have a baby your arms. Not that my youngest daughter was all that keen on coming out. I think she took one look and said: "I'm not going out there, it's full of people with funny hats." Then they brought out the forceps and she said: "Okay, okay I get the message. I'm coming."

I think babies are a bit reluctant to come out because they've heard about all those old movies where the first thing that happens when you are born is some nurse hits you on the rump. Those were the days. Welcome to the world – whack! It's no wonder we live in a violent society. I don't think they do the whack bit any more. It hasn't been necessary with any of our children. They were all born crying. This might be because one of the first things they saw was their father in a shower cap and mask. That sight would make anyone cry.

75. Children

Whoever invented children must have had a wicked sense of humour. The whole process is a crazy ride that takes you from the heights of joy to the lows of sleep deprivation. Nature has hardwired us to breed and protect our young. This defies logic and is not for the faint-hearted.

At each stage of the child's development you reach a milestone, only to be confronted with a new, apparently insurmountable challenge a few weeks later. For example, you think you have found utopia when the baby starts sleeping through the night. But soon after, they start growing teeth and the whole midnight corridor walking starts over again. I suspect the human body's teething system was a last-minute rush job in nature's design. To meet some deadline or other it was thrown together in a hurry without any real thought – cheap parts, not enough room, crooked bits and lots of pain. It is fairly hard for the children as well.

Every time a tooth begins to come through, the household hits the siren and goes on full-scale teething alert. You remove loose objects from the yard, fill the bath with water and buy batteries for the old transistor radio. It begins with the teething groan. The teething groan is the most jarring sound known to man. It makes fingernails on a blackboard sound like Gershwin.

Parents seem to have an in-built tuning system that makes our ears particularly susceptible to the teething groan. Hence, there was a case some years ago when a woman stayed asleep while a truck demolished half her house, but woke up a few minutes later when the baby started crying.

When the baby is teething you have no choice but to respond, regardless of the time of night and how much sleep you have had. Babies expect their parents to fix their pain. At this stage in their lives you don't want to disappoint them. There will be plenty of time for that later. There are quite a few teething remedies available. We feel better trying these even though, deep down, we are fairly sure none of them actually works. The baby probably just gets so tired from all the remedies that it eventually falls asleep, regardless of the pain.

The known remedies include pain-killing fluid, singing Wiggles songs, and those rusk things that look and taste like miniature chair legs. The thing that seems to work best is teething gel. You're supposed to put this on the baby's gums to kill the pain. I find it works better if you put it in your ears. That way your ears go totally numb and you can't hear a thing.

When a baby is teething, it looks for something to gnaw on to help ease the pain. Luckily, nature has provided just the thing: father's finger. Hanging by your side, your finger is at perfect munch height. You can be standing there minding your own business when suddenly "grmmp" ... you are got. To make matters worse, when you finally extract your finger and jump around the room shaking it and inventing new steps for the Macarena, the baby gets the giggles. All babies believe pain is funny, provided it is being experienced by someone else. If they find something that causes pain and Macarena dancing, they like to do it over and over.

Of course, when the household goes through its teething phases, everyone's sleep is affected, including that of the siblings. Some years ago, after my youngest daughter had a long session of teething the night before, I found my son (then four) sprawled out on the couch. "Are you tired mate?" I asked. "No, he replied, "I just ran out of gas."

By then my son had also come to regard his younger sister as something of mess monster, stalking the house like a midget Godzilla. His bedroom was a wonderland of cars, Lego, batman, dinosaurs – the ultimate toddler mess challenge. To keep his sister at bay, my son developed door habits which closely resembled those of Kramer from the *Seinfeld* sitcom. We could follow his progression through the house by the sounds of rapidly opening and shutting doors. On occasions when the toddler broke through his defences and got into his room, he just stood in the middle and screamed. With good reason. Within minutes the whole thing looks like a scene from Twister.

Any household with a mobile baby has a baby chaos zone. This is any area of the house which is within reach of the baby. When you first bring the bundle of bunny rugs and booties home, the chaos zone is negligible – barely a few centimetres either side of where they are laying. It begins to expand when they start rolling around the floor, reaches full room proportions when they begin to crawl, and blows right off the geographical scale once they are upright and learn to use their legs.

Households with upright babies need to be fortified in the same way as *Lord of the Rings* kingdoms fortified against Orks. Locks go on cupboards, pot plants are banished outside, barricades go across important no-go areas, and demilitarised zones are declared where the baby's presence becomes a matter of day-to-day negotiation. The baby brain, which is still being developed, sends out only three signals: Eat, pee and destroy. Sometimes it gets confused and sends all three out together, which results in a trail of moisture, mangled food and general mayhem which can make an ordinary family room look like the *Texas Chainsaw Massacre*.

Toddlers seem particularly drawn to bookshelves. This could be their deep instincts attracting them to intellectual stimulation. More likely it is pretty colours and pictures attracting their "destroy" signals. Babies eye off the bookshelf pretty much from the day they come home from the hospital. When the attack finally comes, it is highly premeditated and exercised with military precision. Before the parental rescue team can be activated, *The Complete Works of William Shakespeare* becomes the *Incomplete Works of William Shakespeare*, *The Fall of Imperial China* is without the entire Ming Dynasty, and Brisbane's southside has been exorcised from the UBD.

Then they discover the fridge. The fridge is the Holy Grail for newly upright babies. It is a place of mystery, of wonder; of potential destruction on a grand scale. Whenever you open the fridge, your eyes and those of your toddler lock into a knowing stare. The toddler has already estimated the distance they must travel to reach the door. The parent is already calculating how quickly they can open the door, locate the food, remove it and restore the barricade before the toddler force breaches the fortress. As the stare breaks, the race is on.

Never underestimate a baby in full flight with an open fridge in its sights. It has the speed of a cheetah, the spring of a taipan and the sheer dogged tenacity of a pit pull. A father desperately grasping for the milk is no match. Soon apples are flying across the floor like hand grenades, fruit yoghurt is spraying blob confetti, and you must dive and execute a classic catch to avoid scrambled eggs on the floor.

When my youngest daughter was a toddler, I was sitting on the lounge chair when I heard an unfamiliar yonder melody. It was a strangely haunting and somehow gripping sound. Then, as my ears properly tuned in, the full horror of the situation suddenly struck me: "The baby has the good dinner set." Sure enough, there poised in the centre of the room was child number three belting out a tune with the coffee pot and dessert bowls and looking up as if to say: "Look dad, cymbals." I have since learnt that girl babies are born with a form of in-built radar which allows them to track down the good dinner set no matter how well it is hidden. They can do the same with expensive perfume, crystal glasses and jewellery - a skill honed in later life at Myer sales.

As your children grow older, the true reality of how much your life has changed really hits your. You realise that the car is now a taxi and is full of strange and unusual seats that require an engineering degree to fit and will almost certainly give you a sore back. The fridge is now a 24-hour take-away shop and every time you sit in the comfy chair a very sharp toy becomes embedded in your bottom.

Almost from the moment you bring that little bundle of joy into your home you are overcome with the realisation that there are now bigger things in life than money. They are called bills. Your wallet enters an intergalactic black hole from which $50 notes are inexplicably sucked almost as soon as they enter. Suddenly, the committee of two, which once made careful investment decisions about the family finances, is an oligarchy of three. Then four. Then five. The most power in the household is inevitably wielded by the one who screams the loudest at 2am. Sometimes this is the newest baby. Other times it is the father who has tripped on the plastic Ninja Turtle that was left in the hallway.

Very soon, the family shopping expedition, which was once a 10-minute job with one of those plastic baskets, becomes an operation of *Waterworld* proportions. Then there's apparel. Children have this really annoying habit of growing all the time. As a result, you are quickly on first-name terms with the guy who runs the shoe store. For children it is a constant battle to try to wear out the shoes before they outgrow them. Usually the contest is neck and neck. The temptation for parents is to dress their children in large, ugly pieces of clothing that will last a long time. Unfortunately, peer-group pressure dictates that small children must be scale replicas of Paris fashion models and their clothes must have an Italian designer name or be worn by the oddly-named child of somebody famous.

As a result of this pressure, we all go out and buy fitted garments that look great for five days – then the buttons start to pop, the stitching comes undone and the rapidly growing child ends up looking like the Incredible Hulk after the lime-flavoured steroids have kicked in.

Studies often show that transport is the biggest cost associated with having children. This is probably because driving a child around in a car is often the only way to get them to sleep. Hence, 70 per cent of the transport cost is probably associated with driving around the block several hundred times between 1.30am and 2.30am.

Other costs come in the form of disposable nappies. Parents generally set out to avoid disposable nappies, hoping to save the planet from death by nappy pile. This often ends badly. Cloth nappies are a scant defence against the atrocities committed by a baby bottom and quickly turn a colour far removed from white. By the second or third child, most parents are clinging to some obscure piece of research that suggests washing cloth nappies destroys the environment too. Disposable nappies also prevent late-night screaming when bleary-eyed men jab themselves in the finger with the giant pin used to hold the cloth diapers together.

76. Childhood wisdom

One of the great things about having small children is that they really believe you are something special. They think everything you say is very wise, you have the strength of a superhero and you are tall like a giant. Eventually, however, reality sets in.

Tall People Don't Jump

When she was much younger, my oldest daughter believed I knew everything and could do anything. That was until the day I put her hair in a ponytail and stood back to admire my work of art. She looked in the mirror and said: "Don't worry dad, I still love you even though you can't do hair." Ouch.

At the time, my son – who we called Chopper when he was a tiny tot – was still naive enough to think I could solve all problems. Whenever he broke a toy, he delivered it to me with the utmost confidence that I could fix it with sticky tape. For a very young boy, sticky tape is the answer to all of life's ills. When I was teaching him to throw a boomerang, it went straight into a tree. "Can you teach me to throw it into the tree too?" was his enthusiastic response.

Chopper, as a three-year-old, was the household proclaimer. He regularly made announcements with such conviction that everyone would stop to listen. Had he been born 40 years earlier, he would almost certainly have been the guy who said: "Elvis has left the building. Thank you and good night."

Most mornings, at about dawn, he would march into the room, pull back the curtain and announce: "It's morning time. The sun's not gone away any more. Time to get my breakfast." Who was I to argue with that type of logic? Around the same time, Chopper went on his first train ride. On Queensland trains, when they are about to leave a station, a voice announces: "Doors closing, please stand clear". After that, whenever Chopper was about to shut himself in the bathroom he would proclaim: "Doors closing, please stand clear." At dinner parties he emerged from his bedroom to announce to assembled guests: "This program is proudly brought to you by Cadbury chocolates, the best chocolates in the entire world." (I think he might have been watching too much television at that point).

We once took him to the doctor with a sore throat. Being fairly well-versed in things medical, he gave the medico his own diagnosis: "I'm very, very sick because my mummy made me eat pumpkin." This was a popular theme. A few months later Chopper was asked by his aunt if he was feeling sick. The conversation went something like this:

Aunt: Are you not feeling well?
Chopper: No I'm sick because I ate soup.
Aunt: But soup won't make you sick.
Chopper: It was pumpkin soup.

On another occasion, Chopper had to be taken to the doctor because a woodchip flew into his eye at the park. He took the whole thing remarkably well, including the temporary placement of a patch over the eye. After a while, the doctor asked the compliant Chopper if he was okay about the patch. "Yes," he replied. "I'm Long John Silver." He was not always quite that chirpy. Another time he slipped on the hall floor while running and burst into tears. I ran to his aid and asked the usual dumb question: "Are you all right mate?" Suddenly the waterworks stopped and Chopper looked at me a little indignant and declared: "No, naturally I'm very upset."

Then there was the time when Chopper's mum sent him to his room for some sort of misbehaviour. Normally he accepted his punishment with a degree of reservation, but on this occasion he opted for a different tack. He bowled up to her, looked her square in the eye and declared: "Mother, you're fired." Nice try. Upon encountering an Aboriginal busker playing a didgeridoo, Chopper (then aged four) inquired: "Dad, who's that brown guy with the trombone." When we were out driving trying to find a particular house or shop, he used to put his nose against the window and announce: "I'm looking for clues."

His other favourite was being placed in the car, tightening his seatbelt and declaring: "Let's rock and ride." This phrase he borrowed from an animated television program called the *Biker*

Mice from Mars, which was a field of riches for a young boy seeking a language to help him relate to the world. The Biker Mice were three large, hairy mice from outer space who came to Earth to help save it from the evil Plutarkians and inflict considerable merchandise on children. This prompted one of Chopper's most enduring pronouncements. Whenever he walked into a room full of people he would say: "Uh, oh, 'Tarkians'." As a result, all our children became affectionately known as "The Tarkians".

At that age, children also love the movies. They are totally consumed by the dark theatre, the action on screen and the sounds. In Chopper's case, he was also totally consumed by the seats. Really. Our favourite local cinema had fold-up seats that relied on your body weight to stay down. Unfortunately, Chopper was really tiny and just didn't have enough weight to keep the seat down. Every time he sat down, his seat ate him. Over time he learnt to sit on the edge of the seat and stay perfectly still. It he made any sudden movements, the seat swallowed him again, leaving arms and legs protruding at an uncomfortable angle and his startled little head bobbing up through the top. Either that or it tossed him into the air like a trapeze artist, spreading popcorn like summer rain. During one movie, Chopper was particularly taken by the action during a sword fight in which some poor unfortunate copped a sword in the bottom. Chopper jumped straight onto his seat and shouted for the benefit of the whole cinema: "Ah ha, got him in the butt." This brought the house down. Chopper basked in the attention until he realised he had moved suddenly. Then the seat ate him.

77. Passing on wisdom

While many children seem to have been born with an innate wisdom, unfortunately they also rely on parents for this. All parents dread the inevitable day when their children will ask that most difficult of questions: "Where do farts come from?"

Most parents struggle with this question and are embarrassed by it, but deep down they also do not want their children to learn about wind-passing from some cartoon show, magazine, or from their grubby friends behind the shed at school. They should be told about it by their parents – when the time is right.

Fathers generally know this question is coming and have a well-considered answer ready: "Ask your mother." If their mother sends them back to the father, he generally makes up a story about storks delivering farts through the belly button. Otherwise, he might talk about people loving a particular food very much and that love produces wind that is better out than in and better up than down. He might use charts and pictures to explain that and use his own anecdote about his own experiences after a well-intentioned foreign meal.

Some parents can simply not talk about it and will opt to tell them about sex instead.

78. Men as dads

Somewhere hopelessly trapped in the back of my brain is the late Harry Chapin singing *Cats in the Cradle*. He's been there for the past 20 years and I can't get rid of him.

"When you comin' home Dad, I don't know when, but we'll get together then son, you know we'll have a good time then."

Shut up, Harry.

Most fathers in the time-starved express lane of the new millennium are haunted by the late Mr Chapin. His song about children waiting their entire childhood for a bit of fatherly attention cuts at the heart strings and strikes pain into some fairly sensitive nerves.

We all secretly harbour a fear that the day will come when we finally have real time for our children, only to find they grew up while we weren't looking and now "my new job's a hassle and kids have the flu but it's sure nice talkin' to you, Dad, it's been sure nice talkin' to you".

Shut up, Harry.

Yep, fathers feel guilty too. Really guilty. In an age where it is accepted as a scientific fact that most men are bastards, it comes with the territory. Always at work; neglecting the family; never there for the children; watching too much sport on television; drinking too much beer. We know, we know. And, as if we need further reminding, the stereotype of the workaholic absent father is reinforced in every second Hollywood movie. Teary, small boy with baseball bat stares forlornly at the spectator stand. Dad didn't make it again. Too busy for his son! Rotten bastard! Of course, Hollywood movies can generally solve these problems in a couple of hours (four hours if the movie is directed by Kevin Costner). In the real world, the problems are more complicated.

While much has been made of the growth in dual-income households and the stampede of post bra-burning women into the workforce, in most traditional-style families, men still assume the role of chief breadwinner. And, for most, it is a tougher part to play than at any time in recent history. At the same time as women were attracting a lot of attention as they became "supermums", by trying to juggle their traditional family responsibilities with paid work, men were finding something unnerving was happening at the office or factory.

Long hours had become expected as we tried to keep up with the hard-working Chinese, roads were clogged, trains and buses were full, there were four out-of-hours functions a week and everyone was competing for the same promotion so they could buy a better house in a better suburb. Suddenly men were eating more meals at the desk than at the dining table and spending more time sitting in the work chair than sleeping in a bed.

There wasn't much choice really. Everywhere we were globalising, corporatising, downsizing and computerising so we could compete with Third World countries where people were forced to work for a dollar a day and a bowl of two-minute noodles. The message at work was clear: "Work harder, you rotten bastards."

So, home went poor Dad, a little dazed and bewildered and exclaimed: "You wouldn't believe what's happened in there…" But before you could mumble "kryptonite", supermum would cut him off and say: "Where have you been, you lazy bastard, don't you know your kids need father time? Tommy's started playing with Barbie dolls, Mary wants to join a commune and the baby's first words were something about the charter of children's rights."

But, but, but…

Modern times can be a hostile environment for fathers. The expectations, financial, emotional and practical, are greater than ever. The onus is on us to become sensitive, new-age, successful nappy-changing machines who do the washing up without expecting praise and go to work for only 30 hours a week to earn $300,000 a year to provide for the Nintendo, Nike and private school needs of our children, who also require 20.75 hours of "quality time", in order for you to avoid a later-in-life litigation seeking substantial damages for ruining their lives. There might also be a book.

Mothers, of course, have their own reasons for feeling under siege (that's why they invented Germaine Greer). But in the angst-filled world of the supermum backlash, fathers are often the unwitting victims of friendly fire. Most of the gender-related writings of the past two decades tend to leave you with a clear impression that men are a pack of clumsy bludgers swanning down at the pub while their womenfolk do all the real work. In fact, at home and at work everyone is working hard. Golf? Recreation? You must be kidding. Get back to the laundry in case those blokes from the NapiSan ad show up and want to film the underwear.

But the upside is that in less than three decades (and here I run the risk of some unfair generalisations), fathers have evolved from often aloof, detached, authoritarian patriarchal breadwinners to slightly more human characters who crave and expect real time with their children. There's no more hanging outside the labour ward handing out cigars. You're in there now taking pictures and giving the commands to breathe.

It is taken as given for most couples that the job of a young father will entail nappy changes and a good share of the midnight baby-rocking hall walks humming Harry Chapin songs.

"But there were planes to catch and bills to pay. He learned to walk while I was away."

I'm warning you, Harry.

I can't speak for all fathers but I suspect most genuinely want more time with their children and have taken up the guilt expected of them. They don't want to miss the milestones and they harbour real fears that they will be regarded as optional extras in an era where people demand free steak knives with every purchase. But equally, they are living in a material world and their daughters are material girls (or sons material boys but that doesn't rhyme as well). To sacrifice the spoils of the full-time working world (and the family opportunity costs that now come with it), also means consigning your family to a lower standard of material living.

There is nothing wrong with that, per se. But peer pressure is a fact of a modern child's life. As much as you try to instil the importance of non-material values, all parents, deep down, do not want their children ever to feel second rate or deprived. Saddled with the responsibility for bringing them into a world which is increasingly insecure, it is often difficult to draw a correct line between time and finances.

And, while there has been much warm and fuzzy rhetoric over the past decade about family-friendly workplaces, few exist. The corporate world is tough and competitive and no company gets an even break because it has a crèche to support. Against this backdrop, fathers are facing an inadequacy crisis as they aspire to be superdads. Their ingrained instincts to be good providers are challenged by a new family-friendly imperative which is often inconsistent with the striving for workplace and monetary success.

In a world grappling with yet another economic downturn, our survival override is giving workplaces the upper hand. But the battle is not yet over. Unfortunately, the childhood often is. "He'd grown up just like me, my boy was just like me."

Enough already Harry, we get the picture!

79. Men in hostile territory

Australian scientists announced some years ago that the oldest stars in the galaxy were in fact 5 billion years younger than they previously let on. This goes to show you should never trust a star. Obviously they were trying to score extra birthday presents and a premature telegram from the Queen. The scientists, yet again, failed to realise the true significance of their discovery. They thought they had learned something boring about the ultimate destruction of the cosmos. What they really did was prove once and for all that the universe is female. No woman would claim to be older than she really was.

Tall People Don't Jump

This is just one of the many examples of the vast differences between the male and female brain. Generally speaking, men and women have nothing in common. In fact,
it is increasingly obvious that when a man and a woman look at the same thing, they see something completely different. For example, when men look at a shopping centre, they see uncomfortable crowds, pushy salespeople and car park spaces fit only for Tonka toys. Women see incredible bargains, clothes to die for and lots of things they must have because there's no way they will ever be at that price again.

The kitchen used to be the same. Women saw it as a place of power, of artistic endeavour and culinary creations. Men saw it as the room where you made toast and cheese. In the new millennium all that has changed. Women now see the kitchen as a symbol of male oppression. They refuse to go in there barefoot, if at all. As a result, men are moving into the kitchen in droves. Generally they leave just as quickly. It's dangerous in there. There are hot things, breakable things and indescribable appliance things that don't have any instructions; all stuff that should come with the warning: "Keep out of the reach of men."

But in there we must go. It's either that or a staple diet of chicken nuggets and those rubber hotdogs they heat up at service stations. In fact, it took the invention of the microwave for it to be considered safe enough for men to enter kitchens. Even now they probably shouldn't go in there alone or at night. They should also avoid eating anything they don't recognise, or that moves.

The microwave, in theory at least, takes the risk out of cooking. The whole thing is locked up in a lead-lined thermo-nuclear chamber which takes perfectly normal food and turns it into X-file mutations. I find everything I put in a microwave either explodes or comes out looking like ceiling insulation. A couple of weeks ago I made a microwave cake that could be worn under a jacket during war to repel bullets.

I used to think the microwave was good for heating up water for coffee. It is until you put the cold spoon in and the whole lot just erupts out the top and oozes snake-like straight off the bench and into your slipper.

For the truly brave, the alternative to the microwave is the old-fashioned method which involves pots, pans, stoves and the Margaret Fulton cooking encyclopaedia.
The trouble is every recipe seems to have two ingredients that I have never heard of or which certainly do not appear in our pantry. As a result, I sometimes do substitution. I figure as long as it is roughly the same colour it probably does the same thing. But be careful. I once used self-raising flour instead of plain flour to make pancakes and they came out looking like swimming drug cheats.

The real enlightenment from my forays into the kitchen has been the discovery of Bicarb (that's the jargon us kitchen types use for bicarbonate of soda). What a product! If you go to the home handy hints section of a book store it is full of publications which basically take 200 pages to tell you to use Bicarb for everything. It is reputed to remove stains, suck out odours, cure arthritis, do something mysterious to scones, stop doors creaking, shine silver and discourage insects.

80. The plastics cupboard

Almost any little mistake you make in life seems to keep coming back to haunt you. With me it is the rogue fork in the cutlery drawer. I once tried to use it to uncork a bottle of red wine. Unfortunately, forks are no good for uncorking wine. As a result, its prongs are rippled and distorted, its handle is bent at an unnatural angle and, in dull light, it has an eerie and unnatural aura about it. Sometimes it looks at me funny.

But I can't bring myself to throw it away. After all, it wasn't its fault I mangled it on the cork. The least I can do is care for it so it can lead a life as close to that of a normal fork as possible. The only trouble with this bit of goodwill on my behalf is that this sad example of forkdom has an uncanny habit of popping up everywhere.

Every second night when I plunge my fork into the peas and carrots they disperse all over the plate. At this point I realise I have the rogue fork (which is no longer capable of picking up food). Occasionally, when we have guests over for dinner, someone screams as their roast potatoes bounce two places away or the tomato zonks them in the eye. I never need to look. I know they have the fork. I make apologies and take the fork back to its drawer. The last thing it would want is pity. But it remains the ghost of my kitchen past.

Kitchens tend to be full of rogue items you can't bring yourself to throw away. There is the bread maker that seemed like a good idea, but you only used twice. There is the ice cream machine that makes great ice cream, if you could just find the booklet that told you how. Every kitchen also seems to have one of those long white things you got as a "free gift" at 1970s Tupperware parties that are used for removing items that fall into the bottom of long-necked bottles. But just how often do you drop things into long-necked bottles? I don't think I have ever in my lifetime seen anyone drop anything into a long-necked bottle. But you keep that white spoon gadget anyway because you can't bring yourself to throw it away. And it was free.

Food is the same. Most kitchen cupboards are full of tins of peeled tomatoes and dodgy soup combinations that passed their use-by date in 1973. But it's kind of comforting to know they are there just in case there is a big flood and you end up spending the night on the roof with a wet possum, a carpet snake and the neighbour's budgie. You still couldn't eat the stuff but it's much better for your peace of mind when the water is swirling around you to have lots of food nearby. Then you are not tempted to eat the budgie.

I find our kitchen cupboards are a bit like the Bermuda Triangle. You go shopping, put things in there and you never see them again. There is a flash of white light and they just sort of blend in with all the rest of the stuff waiting for the flood.

The real shocker in the kitchen, however, is the plastics cupboard. Most plastics cupboards have about two and a half times more plastic things than you can actually fit in the cupboard. As a consequence, every time you open the door, most of the contents spill onto the floor. In keeping with the general kitchen theme, no kitchen plastics are ever thrown away. Every plastics cupboard is like a synthetic museum with items from every historical era and every task and style.

I recently created a new section in our cupboard which is known as PWP – Plastics Without Partners. This is like a singles club for containers that have either been inexplicably divorced from their lids or have lost them in tragic circumstances on the heating element in the dishwasher. I'm thinking of taking my rogue fork to the plastic cupboard in the hope it might meet a nice lidless tumbler and settle down in a sunny spot at the back of the appliance shelf.

Consumption

81. Something to chew on

Almost all humans at several stages in their lives will decide they need to eat better. This generally happens at New Year, when we feel compelled to turn over a new leaf and produce resolutions. These resolutions seldom last more than a week.

Of course, the problem with watching your diet is that it appears pretty much everything is bad for you. For every study that says you should eat something, there is at least one other that says it is bad for you. In the end, the stress of worrying about it all generally kills you before the obesity and cholesterol.

For a start, we are told we should eat food with low fat. However, when we switch to this food we find that the fat has been replaced with sugars and salt. This will also kill you.

We are told to stick to natural products, like fruit. But then we find fruit also has sugar that rots our teeth, and is mostly sprayed with chemicals that are bad for us – same problem with wholemeal and vegetables. Wholemeal has more fibre, but also more chemicals. Vegetables are good, but when you boil them, all the nutrients escape into the water. That's if all the metals in your saucepan and frying pan don't kill you first.

Alcohol either kills you or makes you live forever, depending on which advice you are taking. Juice starts out good, but all the goodness is gone by the time you get it. Cereals are good for you in theory, but most of the ones you buy are full of sugar and bad for you. Health bars have more fat than non-health bars (and lots more sugar). Bottled water has less goodness than tap water, but costs a lot more. At least most foods seem to have lots of energy. But I'm not sure you can actually eat energy.

Butter is a natural food source, but full of cholesterol and fat that will kill you. As an alternative, you can eat margarine, except it might also contain fat and be bleached yellow from its natural black colour, and this may be bad for you.

Curiously, nature seems to have gotten things totally arse about when it comes to humans and food. In a cruel joke on the entire race, the foods we crave and that taste the best are nearly always bad for us. The most nutritious and body-friendly food we can eat is broccoli. Unfortunately, eating broccoli is about the same taste sensation as eating a dish cloth. The next best is brussel sprouts. These taste like rolled-up blotting paper.

As a result of this, when we are really hungry we tend to head straight for a fast-food outlet for some instant calorie gratification. Luckily, most of these outlets now have healthy options and some meals with the Heart Foundation ticks. We usually ignore these and buy hamburgers, but we feel better knowing the healthy choices are there.

82. Coffee

Humans are a little awkward about meeting someone just for the sake of meeting them. A meeting is far more viable when it involves coffee. During the 1990s the human relationship with coffee suddenly blossomed into a full-blown passionate affair. Coffee shops sprung up on every street corner and the aroma of blended beans wafted through the city streets like the call of the siren.

At the same time, coffee became more complicated. In the past we just ordered a cup of coffee. This usually came in a clear glass jug and tasted like the sump oil from a 1950s Valliant. But at least it was easy to order. With specialist coffee shops, suddenly we had lots of choices. A traditional coffee became known as the flat white. We added froth to form the cappuccino. Then there was latte, espresso, mocha, breva, americano, café au lait, macchiato, lungo, ristretto and dopio. We could get coffee with low-fat milk or soy. We could get decaffeinated. We could have it with a twist of caramel or vanilla. Suddenly, we could walk into a coffee shop and order a half-strength, skinny, decaf, soy latte with a twist and no-one would bat an eyelid.

The emergence of the coffee culture has run counter to almost every other development in western society. As time poverty has gripped our civilisation, we are doing almost everything faster. With coffee, we have gone from putting a tea spoon of granules into a cup and adding boiling water (i.e. instant coffee) to complicated formulas that take ages to make. We have gone from needing just a jug and a jar of granules to needing a giant machine with knobs and guzzling sounds that requires an engineering degree to operate. Being trained to operate one of these machines takes about the same time as it takes to train an airline pilot. And you have to get it just right. Everyone is an expert on coffee.

The coffee meeting has added a much-needed new dimension to social interaction. It is the safest of all human meetings because it is never, under any circumstances, considered a "date". It can therefore be used to meet business contacts, catch up with old friends of either gender, hold discussions with work colleagues, or see a relative. The coffee meeting almost never goes for more than an hour and the ordering of the coffee provides a useful starting point to break the ice. You can also use it to impress people by ordering a particularly complicated coffee blend. This confirms you are a person of the world and very cultured. This is particularly the case if you can talk with authority about the origin of the beans.

Coffee can also be used for strategic body language manoeuvres during difficult business discussions. If someone says something at the coffee meeting that you disagree with, you can take a sip from your coffee and slightly raise your eyebrows. This leaves a slightly uncomfortable pause in which the other person might add a qualification like "of course we are flexible on this" or "we can do it another way if you would prefer". You can also stare thoughtfully into the coffee cup when you are thinking about a response. This sends a message that you are a deep thinker and capable of seeing wisdom in the cup.

It is fairly easy to look cool while you are drinking coffee. The exception to this is when you go in too early and it is too hot. Even if you burn your lips, you have to pretend that the coffee is fine. Once you acknowledge that you have burnt yourself with coffee, the other person will just think you are a dufus. You cannot recover from that. Nothing good ever came from being a dufus.

Coffee represents a great business opportunity because the price people are prepared to pay for a good coffee is vastly more than the cost of making it. People will fork out $5 or more for a coffee, even though deep down they know it is worth nowhere near that much. We assume, however, that an expensive coffee must have some special quality to it. This might have something to do with the origin of the beans, or the tone of the gurgling sound made by the machine, or the fact that the person making it is called a barista and often has a certificate to prove it.

83. Alcohol

In many respects, coffee has taken over some of the role of alcohol in human society. When the corporate landscape was almost entirely dominated by men, business discussions often happened over a "drink".

Frequently this was more than just a meeting. It was a ritual of manhood with origins dating back to medieval duals. This involved one businessman being able to drink the other businessman "under the table". In other words, this was a test of how much alcohol someone could consume before they became paralytic. The correlation between being able to consume vast quantities of alcohol and business partnership prowess was never entirely clear. Many deals, however, were struck on the basis of the mutual respect developed in this way.

In the new millennium, alcohol still plays a very strong role in societal interaction, but far less so in the business environment. Drink-driving has become a major don't-do criminal activity rather than the minor social faux pas of 30 years ago. Being under the influence of liquor in the workplace is highly frowned upon, particularly as it often leads to harassment, bullying and vomiting into pot plants. Women are also adverse to the drink-under-the-table corporate dealing culture and have ushered in far more civilised workplaces full of equal opportunity, anti-harassment legislation and cafe lattes. This is generally considered a good thing.

Outside of work, however, alcohol remains an important social lubricant. People also find alcohol very funny. Almost any reference to alcohol and any social situation will produce laughter. If you are at a conference and anyone makes reference to drinking too much, you can guarantee a laugh. If you are having a morning meeting and you make reference to someone having "a few too many" the night before, that is also a guaranteed laugh. If you mention dealing with any social problem with alcohol, that is also funny. Mention that someone "likes a drink" and there will be laughs all-round.

The alcohol-laughter nexus appears to be a link between the golden age of slapstick comedy and the fact that people who have consumed too much alcohol tend to stagger and fall over a lot. People who have drunk too much also slur their speech, even though in their own minds they are speaking with perfect clarity. Sometimes they get aggressive and tell the boss what they really think of them. This is seldom flattering, and may not be so funny when you front for work the next day.

Shopping

84. Shop (till you drop)

The hunting and gathering of food has changed very little over the course of human history. In the Stone Age they endured wild animals, hostile tribes and occasional clubbings to bring back the family supplies. The modern equivalent is the suburban supermarket.

Doing the family shopping can be a frightening experience. The shops are full of aggressive people brandishing large steel trolleys that cut corners and double-park in the confectionary aisle.

In the shopping environment there are significant differences between men and women. Despite years of practice, most men lack basic shopping skills. Women, on the other hand, can usually spot a bargain from three rows away. Men usually buy the brand with the most impressive label, or one they recognise from the television. They will seldom buy "plain wrap" products which they assume are made in a large, dull, unmarked factory by ordinary-looking people in standard grey overalls, and sent to the shops in plain brown trucks.

One of the most challenging aspects of supermarket shopping is the trolley selection. The trolleys are inevitably jammed together in such a way they can only be parted by a small explosion or Mr Bodybuilder Australia.

All supermarket trolley factories have employed a man with a hammer to bash one of the wheels. This ensures they wobble, squeak and turn in circles rather than go in a straight line. To make matters worse, all supermarket aisles are only 1.95 trolley widths wide. When you need to pass another shopper, clear give-way rules apply. Women should always give way to men because if the guy is doing the shopping, he needs all the help he can get. It also pays to give way to anyone who lived through the Great Depression or the Playtex sales of the early 1970s. This group is particularly aggressive in the shopping environment and should be treated with caution. Do not stand between them and the last loaf of sliced white.

Just to prove the supermarket manager has a sense of humour, he provides things called cart corrals in the car park. These are designed as a place for customers to deposit their trolley after they have unpacked their groceries. In their dreams. These corrals are always about 2.6km from any vacant parking space I have ever found. Returning the trolley to them requires the longest walk since the early explorers. Hence, people just check no-one is watching, give the trolley a shove, jump in the car and speed away before the trolley police with the tractor and long trailer can nab them.

For some reason, trolleys in supermarket car parks look like they have been in the middle of a nuclear explosion. It is as if they have panicked and jumped into gardens, up trees and behind posts. Others are crashed at the bottom of hills or tilted in unnatural positions with one wheel on the gutter. They also seem to have infiltrated the community. The last time I went to the coast, there was a trolley on the beach sunning itself. Trolleys are also in creeks, back yards, at the races and at various festivals and public events.

If you manage to get through the trolley selection and hunting and gathering stage of shopping, the next big challenge is the checkout. The supermarket checkout is one of mankind's most stressful environments. In the good old days, when people were in charge, it wasn't so bad. Now the machines have taken over, it's a sweaty-palm zone.

Take the price scanners. Former United States president George Bush is credited with discovering these scanners during the 1992 presidential election campaign. The rest of the world, of course, discovered them at least five years earlier.

Before scanners, you handed over the product, and a friendly checkout operator would punch in the price and probably talk with you about the weather and her aunt's latest operation. The new system is far more efficient. First they whip the product past the scanner – and nothing happens. Then they put it through really slowly – and nothing happens. Then they swear under their breath and type in a product code number longer than an international phone number. This takes roughly twice as long as it used to take to just punch in the price.

Sometimes the scanner refuses to give a price so the checkout person calls for the dreaded price check. Price checks are feared throughout the Western world. Once they call one, you must cancel any other plans you had for that day, possibly for the whole week. The checkout person usually has to ring her little bell furiously and wave the product around in the air for about 10 minutes trying to attract the attention of someone to check the price. Sometimes they use the microphone to call for help. This is generally ignored. If you are really lucky, someone eventually shows up and takes your product away. If this happens, take a good look at them. You almost certainly will never see them again. Price checks never happen when you are buying anything cool like aftershave or expensive bottled water. They save them for the toilet paper and plain brand underwear.

Some of the worst shopping moments happen around tampons. Tampons are a bit like toilet paper and laxatives in that people (men anyway) generally try to pretend they don't exist. When they are being put through the checkout, the male customer pretends to be deeply engrossed in the impulse chocolate rack. If they inadvertently make eye contact with the checkout operator, they tend to go a little red and feel the need to whisper: "They're not for me."

Back in the good old days of shopping, you paid for your groceries with real money. These days, to avoid muggers, you usually do it through electronic funds transfer. In this process you are at the mercy of two machines – one at the shop and one at your bank. If these machines do not like each other, you are in big trouble.

So you put in your card, type in your top-secret, spy-ring code number and wait. The process is very similar to weightlifters waiting for the lights to tell them they have made a clean lift. The whole thing causes intense interest among those waiting behind you in the checkout line. If there is a long delay waiting for the

machine to answer, they start to whisper: "He's got no money", "Something's gone wrong",
"They're going to take back the groceries".

On good days, it comes up "transaction approved" and the line of people break into spontaneous applause and hug one another. On a bad day, the card lets you down and the groceries must be put back on the shelves. This is a time of great sadness. It is like returning orphans who thought they were chosen.

85. Lying in wait

Even when you have successfully exited the supermarket with the results of your hunting expedition, you are not completely safe. You still must get past the temporary desk in the aisle of the shopping centre, one of the most difficult terrains in retail geography.

These desks are selling everything from cladding to environmental causes and tuition and have only a few days to do it. The occupants are restless and dangerous when cornered. Most shoppers try to avoid eye contact with the centre aisle people and walk past quickly, pretending they have somewhere better to be. Others will get close and give one of those "I've just seen a speed camera" looks and high-tail it in the other direction. The fastest of these generally escape. Sadly, the slow and very polite people in society lack the skills to avoid the temporary desk and often fall victim to it. Their house ends up clad when it didn't need to be, they learn a language they will never use, and they help save a rare African insect that only a mother could love. This is part of the circle of life.

86. Taking it back

Inevitably, after any male shopping trip, at least one item will need to be returned. This is particularly the case if the male has bought a present for the female or used any initiative in the process. Male initiative in a shop always ends badly.

Returning an item to a store may seem like a simple task but, as with any shopping manoeuvre, it is fraught with complications and should not be attempted without adequate training and a confident disposition.

While many retailers boast that they will "cheerfully" provide refunds on things you return, there is little evidence of cheer in that part of the shop. For a start, there is always a long line and nobody looks particularly happy.

The returns counter is where humans go to admit their failures, make good their mistakes and to practice a genuine-and-sincere-excuse face. Yes, we admit, we did buy the item (usually clothing) but it was totally the wrong size, the wrong shape, the wrong sort, the wrong colour – it was just plain wrong. "And today I am here to put it right." Some return counter staff that apparently have no personal attachment to the retailer's money, will just say: "Okay, refund or exchange?" In these cases you are overcome with euphoria. Others will ask questions like: "Didn't you try it on?" This is a dumb question to ask a man. Men don't try things on. We have an innate way of knowing if something will fit. If it doesn't, that is not our fault. We genuinely believed it fitted when we left the store.

Sometimes the counter staff will need to ask a supervisor. This is a very bad sign. The supervisor has no love for the refund or the exchange and they know the rules. Once they call for the supervisor, there will be no refund or exchange. Instead, you will keep the item and give it as a gift to someone smaller. Or someone the same size, who you don't like.

The biggest fear for anyone returning an item is the "send away". The send away is when an item is broken and the store intends sending it away to be fixed. This is always a high-stress situation. For a start, you lose the instant gratification of getting a new item or your money back. Secondly, you never really know where it will be sent or if you will ever see the item again. You fully expect that product you bought, which was probably made in China, will be returned to China on a slow boat which will take many months. By the time you get it back, it either still won't work or you will have totally lost interest in it.

The key to any successful product return is the receipt. The receipt is a powerful document that proves you bought the item from that store. Even a supervisor cannot ignore the receipt. Without the receipt, you are in a much worse position. This requires them to trust you. To get their trust you need an honest face. Most people who try to put on an honest face end up looking like criminals. If this happens, there will be no exchange or refund and you will be lucky to avoid being arrested.

If you manage to successfully convince the store that this product should indeed go back, you will often be given choices – a refund, a voucher or an exchange. Faced with options, you tend to act like you are not particularly bothered which you choose. Deep down, however, you want the refund. The refund allows you to wipe the whole sorry experience from the record and start the whole purchase decision all over. The exchange increases the chances that you will get it wrong again, and the voucher just serves as a reminder of the failed purchase and a requirement for you to return to the scene of the failure to relive the shame.

The highest degree of difficulty in the product return world is the faulty underwear. Once stores have offloaded underwear, they really don't want it back. They are not sure where it has been and they are in no mood to take any chances. There are a few recorded cases of successful underwear return, but these generally involve chronic knickers malfunction or stitching blowouts caused by poor workmanship. Returned underwear is the most reviled item in the giant plastic box where shop return items are kept. They have been known to contaminate a whole batch.

87. Something smaller

Another thing you quickly notice when you are shopping is that society seems to have developed a serious shortage of change. As a result, shop assistants have been sent on an unrelenting mission to find "something smaller".

If you attempt to buy something worth less than $5 with a $20 note, the shop assistant panics. "Do you have something smaller?" they ask. You immediately start counting coins and rustling through the old dockets looking for the elusive smaller something.

Sometimes you can do it with your collection of five cent pieces. Other times you admit failure. "Sorry," you say. "That's the smallest I've got." At this point the shop assistant gives you a contemptuous look and slowly changes your large note with precious smaller bills. This is done with the gravity of donating a kidney.

And don't even think about producing a $100 bill. Even banks don't like to change those. In fact, if you give almost anyone a $100 note their first instinct is to hold it up to the light to check if it is counterfeit. Most people have never seen a bill this large and may doubt it is real money. They assume you are a bank robber and you have lots more like it at home, in cloth bags with dollar signs on the side.

With modern electronic transfer technology, you can not only buy things at shops, you can also withdraw money from your savings account. Most larger stores will give you up to $1000. Of course, if you actually ask for this amount the shop assistant treats you as if you are robbing the store. The cash will generally have to be brought up from "the office" and everyone seems to be looking at you funny. It is as if the store never really expects you to take them up on the cash withdrawal offer. And now that you have, there just isn't enough money for everybody else. They hope you are happy now.

As environmental concerns become more common, shop assistants are also becoming very protective of their plastic bags. They used to give you a bag for everything. Now they ask if you want one. If the answer is yes, they look at you as if you are personally responsible for global warming and the hole in the ozone layer. They also assume you don't like penguins.

88. Out the back

Another pitfall to avoid when shopping is believing that there is anything "out the back". Out the back is one of the biggest shams in retail. It is used to create an expectation for customers that the item they are looking for, which is clearly not on any shelf, might in fact be in one of the secret areas at the back of the store, where shoppers are not allowed to go.

Even getting to this stage is quite a challenge. Retail staff in large stores generally try to avoid customers so they can get on with stacking shelves and clean-ups in aisle 12. If you manage to engage one of them and ask if they stock a product, their first response is to offer to check out the back.

Smart shoppers know there is nothing out the back. Out the back is just a big empty space created to perpetuate the illusion that there are vast expanses of products ready for purchase and the things that are on show are just a small cross-section of what you can buy. I'm fairly sure that what really happens in these circumstances is the retail worker walks out the back, counts to 20 and returns to let you know there are none out the back either.

Animals

89. Whales

Most humans love whales and claim to have a spiritual relationship with them. The exception to this is Japanese, who eat them for scientific purposes. Humans know that whales are large and smart. They are also mammals rather than fish, and this is apparently significant and worth repeating a lot.

We are so obsessed with whales that we have created a whole industry around watching them. We don't even choose to disguise this. It is known as the whale watching industry. The whales must find this fairly freaky; boatloads of tourists just watching them. This almost certainly causes giant whale nightmares and phobia. "Why are they watching me?" the giant whale brain thinks.

While whales are generally passive and try to avoid humans who are freaking them out, people are also secretly fearful of them because of their sheer size. There have been isolated cases over the years of people being eaten by whales. The most famous is the story of Jonah in the Bible. Less well known is the tale of British sailor James Bartley who was working on a whaling boat in 1891 when a rogue whale smashed through the bottom of the boat, creating mayhem for the crew. Somewhere in the confusion, Bartley disappeared.

Later, the whale died and was hauled on board to be carved up for blubber and oil. During the butchering process someone noticed movement in the stomach and out popped Bartley, freaking everybody out. The ship's doctor told the crew to tip buckets of sea water over Bartley. It is not clear why he ordered this but no doubt it was fairly annoying for a man who had just spent a fair while in a whale's stomach.

There is some disagreement over what happened next. Some say after three weeks of recuperation he returned to normal and went back to sea. Others say he went blind, his hair fell out, his skin turned deathly white and he became a boot maker. Either way, he turned his back on lucrative book deals and television appearances. This was partly due to television not yet being invented.

90. Dogs

Comedian Sue Murphy noted that humans will sometimes walk into a room and forget why they are there. She suggested that dogs spend their whole lives doing that. The world appears to be divided equally between dog people and non-dog people. Some non-dog people are cat people. Cat people often hate dog people. Some cat people are cat people *and* dog people. In extreme cases, they are animal people and their homes look like a zoo.

I have always liked the concept of a dog, but I have generally been put off by the poop collecting during walks in public places. This seems to significantly offset the advantages of having a creature to collect your slippers and your paper. I think this makes me a non-dog person. Even so, I have been an astute observer of dogs for many years and I have seen a couple of dog movies, including the *Lassie* remake.

Even after years of observations I am not entirely clear whether dogs are really smart or entirely mentally challenged. In this, television is no help whatsoever. On television, dogs are always really brave and smart. They will dive into creeks to rescue people, fetch help when there is a problem and they pretty much never poop. However, if you observe carefully, the humans on the dog television shows are the real heroes. They actually talk dog. The dog can come running into the house and start barking and the exchange will go something like this:

Dog: (Excitedly) Woof, woof, woof.

Human: Slow down boy, what is it?
Dog: (Slightly less excitedly) Woof, woof, woof.
Human: Oh no, Jimmy has fallen down the old mine on McNally's farm. Let's go boy.

Curiously, television almost never makes shows about hero cats. Cats are generally depicted as lazy and self-indulgent. This would seem to suggest that television is highly dominated by dog people. Most US Presidents also seem to be dog people. Dog people have permeated deep into our civilisation. One day, dogs might take over the world. This would almost certainly see a relaxation in public urination laws.

In real life, the behaviour of dogs is a bit harder to gauge. For example, when you walk or jog down the street in the morning, just about every dog you pass starts barking. Why is this? What is the dog thinking? Is the message to me: "You better keep walking down that street or I'll come out there and deal with you"? Or is it thinking "how dare you walk down that street". Does it even know it is fenced in and tied up? Or is it all bark, and no bite, and sitting in there hoping that you keep walking and it does not have to follow through on the threat?

If dogs are challenging your right to walk down the street, wouldn't they be living their lives with a complete sense of failure? They must think: "I bark every time someone walks down the street but the same people keep walking down the street. I can't be very good at this."

And what about the dogs who bark at the postman every day? Wouldn't they, after a while at least, start to think that perhaps the postman, despite some ugly postal worker gun incidents overseas, is fairly harmless? Or do dogs just not like letters? Or perhaps bills? Maybe they are really barking at the bills and not the postman. But, if so, how do they know bills are bad? Dogs don't usually have to pay bills.

And why do dogs always start barking when other dogs bark? Are they talking to each other in a secret dog language? Or is it more evidence of the dog inferiority complex: "Rex is barking. There must be something to bark at. I must bark too. Bark, bark, bark."

You also have to wonder, if dogs just bark at anything, is the barking really having any impact. I fear that in real life, if poor Jimmy fell down the mine, the poor little bugger would be down there for quite some time.

91. A tangled web

Social history has, for reasons unclear, required men to be tough and fearless in most situations. Genetics and the male brain has never really caught up with this, so men have to spend a lot of time pretending they are fearless when inside they are scared witless.

This is mostly starkly demonstrated in dealing with household spiders. All men (except fit, skinny men who wear long shorts, brimmed hats and know about the bush and stuff) are secretly terrified of spiders. If a spider falls on their hand or on their head while they are by themselves they will jump around in panic, brushing the affected area wildly and screaming "get it off, get it off". In company, this is not an option. In these circumstances they remain calm and controlled and simply brush the spider off or kill it with a book. Of course, inside their head their brain is panicking, sending out urgent signals to brush the affected area wildly and scream "get it off, get if off".

In spider land, the bigger the spider, the less poisonous they seem to be. This doesn't help them much when they encounter a human male. Human males have only one instinct when it comes to a large, hairy, ugly spider – kill, and from as far away as possible.

For men, the worst place to have to deal with a spider is when it is on the ceiling and a woman is watching. The ceiling is an unpredictable place for spiders because their speed and cunning mixes with gravity. At any time they can run and fall. In the split second after you whack a spider on the ceiling you don't really know where it is. It could be in your hair, on your neck or crawling down your back. At this point, regardless of where the spider is, almost every surface of your body feels like there is a spider on it. Your brain is telling you to jump around and brush wildly. Your ego is saying: "You must impress this woman. It is only a spider. Act cool man."

This represents another interesting internal battle for human males. The brain will ultimately win the contest, but the ego will try very hard, and go down fighting.

92. Insects

We are all told as children that if there is a nuclear holocaust, the cockroaches will survive. This is accepted by pretty much everyone as a fact. Thinking about it, it is not entirely clear what gives cockroaches their special nuclear survival capacity. Humans can easily kill cockroaches with a shoe. Does that mean shoes are more powerful than nuclear explosions?

Another commonly-accepted scientific fact is that, if humans became extinct, insects would be the next dominant species. This is a very sobering thought. An insect world would be very creepy and very bad for dogs, which would have no means to control the fleas. Inevitably, bugs would also get bigger and start to look like the alien bugs from *Starship Troopers* which made loud freakish noises and sucked out people's brains, something that looked particularly unpleasant.

Individually, insects aren't particularly impressive. Ants, for example, boast that they can lift 10 times their body weight. But who cares? They weigh basically nothing. Ten times their body weight is only slightly more than nothing. Big deal. Ants can, however, make quite an impression in large numbers and build impressive mounds. This is the ant equivalent of the pyramids. In the ant world there is probably widespread conjecture about how the mounds are built, and some ants would suggest aliens were responsible.

The life of an ant is fairly fragile, and often they are stood on or eaten by predators. They have a firmly entrenched class system where the Queen is all-powerful, there are a few flyers and the rest are workers or drones. Being a drone in the ant kingdom is one of life's ultimate bummers. It is hard enough being an ant but being a drone as well gives you few prospects in life.

93. Fear of vermin

One of my favourite Gary Larson *Far Side* cartoons has God rolling up clay to make snakes. "These things are a cinch," he declares. Yes, when it comes to design and accessories, the snake dipped out badly. It was standing behind the proverbial door when the cool stuff like legs, arms and hair were handed out.

What's more, snakes scare the heebeejeebees out of everyone. Most of the things in life that we fear derive their fear factor from what we are taught as children. Snakes are different. We are all born with an innate desire to hit them over the head with a lump of wood.

To protect snakes from their natural lack of popularity, nature has supplied them with poison and speed. This gives them the option of killing things or sliding away from them. Sometimes, they slide away so fast they leave their skin behind. Generally, while they are sitting there thinking about whether to slide or kill, someone hits them over the head with a lump of wood.

Thinking is particularly hard for snakes because they don't have any fingers to scratch their heads. More recently, governments also have introduced laws to protect snakes. It is now illegal to kill them unless they are about to bite you or they are holding up a liquor store.

This has deprived Australian males of one of their great tests of manhood. Australian suburban folklore is awash with tales of ordinary dads who took on the king brown or the red-belly black with just a garden rake or a lump of "4by2".

Now all dads can do is say "shoo". It is very hard to look tough when you are saying "shoo". There are no suburban legends about shooing. People do not sit around the bar boasting about a particularly successful shoo.

Even so, families still look to fathers for wisdom about the snake. All children have questions about snakes and they seek out their fathers for answers. My son is no exception. When we were walking along the beach when he was very young he asked whether there were snakes in the water. Not wanting to scare him, I assured him there were no snakes on the beach. Five minutes later we nearly stood on one.

Some years later we were hiking around a river near the Australian capital Canberra. That day we had been discussing snakes and I assured the children there was nothing to worry about in that part of the river. Sure enough, a little while later down the river floated a large, black, ugly, menacing serpent.

Now the children seek all snake wisdom from their mother.

New Zealanders particularly do not like snakes and go to enormous lengths to keep them out of their country. I remember being told as a kid that a snake had escaped from a ship in a NZ port and they dismantled half the loading area to find it. Before their sporting teams will play on an Australian field they do a special Maori war dance to scare away any snakes that might have slithered onto the field.

Not that I blame them. I am also particularly cautious about snakes after a dangerous encounter as a child that left me in severe pain. I was hiking up a mountain with a group of kids and adults when I heard a bloodcurdling scream and felt a horrendous, sharp, throb in my foot. A split second later I looked down at the path and there sprawled in front of me was a highly venomous Death Adder. But that was not the cause of the pain. One of the adults walking in front of me had seen it first, screamed and jumped backwards, landing on my foot and badly bruising it.

The snake, realising it had no fingers to scratch its head and think, slithered off down the hill in a mad panic as the dreaded chorus of "shoo, shoo" rang in its ears.

94. Attack from above

To gain an advantage in the theatre of war, you need to control the skies. The same is true of suburbia which, at certain times of the year, is controlled by plovers, magpies and bats. For reasons that are not entirely clear, magpies and plovers choose to breed in the middle of built-up housing areas and then seem surprised when there are people all around them. What's more, despite years of diving at humans and generally giving them a hard time, we are still here. Yet somehow, these birds have failed to come up with a better system.

The attacks from above are a particular dilemma for conservation-minded suburbanites who believe all of God's creatures deserve to live in harmony. This is a hard argument to sustain when creatures with giant beaks are swooping at you and attempting to remove skin, hair and eyes. After a while it really pisses you off.

While the birds don't tend to do a lot of damage, they present real self-image problems for humans. It is really hard to look cool when you are being swooped at by a bird. You have to overcome your natural ducking instinct or wear a giant hat that makes you look like a Mediterranean grape farmer. Some people carry giant sticks or golf clubs. This sometimes ends badly. These people almost never hit the bird and often swing wildly and clunk themselves in the leg. It is also hard to look cool while you are swinging a giant stick at a swooping bird. Footage of this will inevitably end up on one of those funniest home video shows.

Plovers have particular anger management issues and seem to resent their eggs and their offspring. As a species, they have no apparent sense of humour and sound like a trumpet being tortured in a meat grinder. To make it interesting, the plovers lay their eggs in the middle of an open paddock, making them almost impossible to protect. Then they pace around like older men waiting for the urinal and swoop at anything that comes within 400m. Most of the time the plover eggs don't survive. This creates intergenerational resentment that confines this species to enduring agro, like the Middle East.

Bats are different because they come out at night and actually try to avoid you. The trouble is they hang out in little trees and when you walk past, you scare them and they fly straight at you. This might be because they hang upside down a lot and blood runs to their head. This makes them a little groggy when they fly, leaving them prone to poor direction and collision. Bats are particularly creepy when they flock in large numbers. They look like a sinister cloud or extras in an Alfred Hitchcock movie.

Magpies are perhaps the most potent of the lot. They make no noise when they swoop and are perfectly comfortable taking chunks out of your head. The birds seem to have a particular aversion to postal service employees. This is unfortunate because these people already have enough problems.

Popular culture

95. Too cool

Fads and fashion have always been a curiosity to me. One minute something is flavour of the month, the next it is geek horror show and you seek to destroy all of the photographic evidence before it goes viral. Fads also tend to work in extremes; you like a fad or you hate it. You cannot half like a fad. Fads must be exercised as an extreme sport.

Children learn about what is hip at a young age. Fad consciousness is most pronounced at about age 10. Unfortunately, I turned 10 in the 1970s, which was a particularly bad period for cool. Grown men were walking around in open-chested, cheesecloth and using words like "flower power" and "peace, man". Kids had no chance. They grew up with a warped sense of cool from which they would never fully recover.

About this time, I insisted my mother buy the material for the shirts she made me from the curtain section of the fabric store (the only department at the time which seemed to understand cool). My staple wardrobe was green and red swirling floral pattern shirts and a leather shoelace around my neck. The shoelace was the idea of my best mate at the time, Knotty. Knotty was the Year 4 authority on cool. He had the title because he knew the words to one of Billy Thorpe and the Aztecs' songs and he could bend his finger at the first joint.

As I walked around in my floral shirt and shoelace, I knew everyone was looking at me and thinking: "Now that dude is way too cool for school." Looking back on it years later, I suspect they were really thinking: "Why is that dweeb dressed in a curtain and why is there a shoelace around his neck?" Come to think of it, I'm not sure if anyone besides Knotty and I wore the shoelaces. We were obviously ahead of our time. Or maybe our time is still coming. There are still not a whole hell of a lot of people wearing shoelaces around their necks. Poor uncool bastards.

To deviate slightly, and to fully demonstrate Knotty's cool credentials, later that year we had starring roles in the class Christmas play. I got to play Santa because my mother made me a red suit. Knotty played the child in the family because he had his own Christmas stocking which he was allowed to bring along.

My big scene was when I did a simulated drop down the chimney. It was a low-budget production so this entailed jumping in the air once and doing a slight wriggle that indicated going down an actual chimney. Then disaster struck. The presents I had brought along as props were all large things, like books and stuffed toys. Alas, Knotty's stocking, by comparison, was tiny with an opening meant for little toys and candy. As hard as I tried, none of the presents would go in. So I gave up and jumped on my simulated sleigh and headed back to the North Pole, following a cardboard sign on a tree that said "North Pole".

Suddenly, Knotty, who had been doing a great job of pretending to be asleep, jumped up and delivered his big line: "It's morning and look at all the presents Santa brought." Then he looked at his stocking and, with the greatest look of surprise I have ever seen on anyone's face, added: "Ooh, none!"

This really wrecked the next scene when he was supposed to show the new toys to his "parents" (other class members dressed in op-shop clothing). I think he ad-libbed some line about Santa having a nasty accident.

But back to fads. The other biggies at the time were French knitting, click-clacks and yo-yos. Yo-yos weren't my specialty. Knotty could make his hum the national anthem and draw

Tall People Don't Jump

pictures in the air. Mine just went up and down. Sometimes just down.

French knitting, on the other hand, was more my scene. I could wield a cotton reel and bobby pin with the best of them. There was a fair bit of competition at the time to produce the longest continuous stream of French knitting. I'm not sure why. When you are 10, these things seem to matter. Mind you, at the time it also mattered whether Gilligan got off the island and if Marcia Brady was going to need braces. It is not until age 14 you learnt not to give a rat's arse about anything that doesn't cost you or bite you.

My giant ball of knitting became legendary. I was stopped in the playground by older kids seeking tips on technique and economy of stroke. People would seek confirmation of the length of the French knitting. Some doubted it. But the legend grew. After a while I stopped bringing it to school. However, in the minds of the other children, it was still growing. Each time they told the story, the knitting rope was longer and longer. Some people believed it would reach the moon.

Unfortunately, nothing lasts forever. After a few months the fad passed and I became just another face in the crowd with a thoroughly useless 50m ball of knitting in my bag that wouldn't reach the fence, much less the moon. I kept it for years in case the fad returned. It didn't. Few do.

Click-clacks were another inexplicable 1970s things that seemed to have no particular reason for existing. They were basically two balls on a string which was attached to a handle. If you moved the handle up and down, the balls went into a frenzy and knocked against each other, producing a noise like woodpeckers on steroids. If you lacked co-ordination, the balls smashed into your limbs, causing brusing. After a few minutes of click-clacking, you started to ask yourself: "What have I achieved here?" I had no idea.

96. The television fixation

For the past 60-odd years, humans have spent a large proportion of their waking hours sitting in their lounge rooms staring at a box known as television. Sadly this is because whatever is on television is usually more interesting than what is happening in their actual lives. There is also occasional nudity and coarse language.

One of the big problems with modern television is that it only seems to be able to handle one idea at a time. In the 1970s it was cop shows. Whenever someone came up with an idea it was a cop show. Anything that wasn't a cop show didn't qualify as an idea. This was the decade of cops.

Most cop shows involve a rebellious cop who makes a lot of arrests but breaks all the rules, smashing cars and keeping scum off the streets. They nearly always have an understanding but frustrated partner and a grumpy, Afro-American chief who threatens in every episode to send the hero's arse back to writing parking tickets outside the library. Sometimes there were supermodel cops who worked for an electronic speaker box known as Charlie, and jiggled a fair bit as they chased suspects. One show was set in Hawaii, known for loud shirts.

In the 1980s it was all family shows that showcased women with perms so large they could be spotted from space. Families in this decade were generally dysfunctional and on drugs.

By the 1990s we were beset with infotainment that told us everything from how to pay our bills to six different uses for manure. In the current hard-to-name decade, there is a battle between reality television and shows about forensic medicine. This may be two ideas, which means one must go.

In the forensic shows, most of the dialogue happens in a room with a dead person whose innards have been largely removed.

Tall People Don't Jump

All the plots seem to be the same, but nobody appears to notice. The dead people in the forensic shows generally have slightly more personality than the reality show contestants.

The other big mover is quiz shows in which people with too much time on their hands battle for money, trips and the car. The quiz show boom raises an important issue: Are we in danger of running out of quiz questions? Presumably there is a limit to how many things people can know. Will we have to start rationing quiz questions so you can only use them on odd days of the week? Will we need slower-talking quiz masters who ask fewer questions during the half hour? Will we need to start importing cheap questions from third-world countries to keep up with the demand?

Another big success is talent quests, which take people from relative obscurity, put them in the public spotlight for a few weeks, and then return them to relative obscurity when the second album fails. This provides current affairs programs with lots of fodder stories about disgruntled former stars. It also saves recording companies finding actual new talent that can be ripped off on the internet.

To encourage people to watch television instead of having a life, stations must constantly promote upcoming shows. The promotions are nearly always better than the actual shows and really should carry footnotes to explain what the promotion really means. If it did, it would look something like this:

1. "For the first time on network television."

Footnote: You have already seen it on video, DVD, pay television, on the free screen in the park and on the aircraft.

Footnote 2: For the first time interrupted every 10 minutes by 15 minutes of commercials.

2. "At the special time of (insert time)."

Footnote: We found something decent to put in its usual time slot so we're putting this rubbish on when no-one is watching.

3. "Before there was (movie currently in cinemas), Actor B made us laugh in (insert old movie you've seen six times). Watch it tonight on (insert channel)."

Footnote: Blatant attempt to snare some ratings by associating old flick with current cinema hit.

4. "In the tradition of (insert very popular movie)."

Footnote: This is a bad B-grade movie, but like the blockbuster *Titanic* it also has water and a ship.

5. "The episode that you've been waiting for."

Footnote: Something actually happens tonight. If you have been watching this rubbish, you have probably been waiting for something to happen.

6. "You decide who stays and goes."

Footnote: No-one is watching this reality TV show any more so if you call and spend $5, you (and you alone) probably will decide who stays and goes.

97. Rock clips and celebrity interviews

Over the years, I have spent a lot of time taking in interviews with actors and rock stars. These interviews fill thousands of magazine pages and take up hundreds of hours of air time. It might be sacrilege to say it, but do these people really have anything to say? In fact, does being able to sing and act automatically give people lots of wisdom to share?

Tall People Don't Jump

Sadly, the answer generally seems to be "no". Actors seem to mostly talk about how happy they are with the "good place" they are in and how great the director and the other actors in their movies are. They make a point of not talking about whom they are dating or anything controversial. They will, however, talk about the products they are endorsing and their upcoming book. Sometimes they will talk about a "cause" like whales. Most of the time they don't seem to know much about the cause but if it is fur they will probably be prepared to pose naked.

During most interviews, rock stars, unless they are Bono or Bob Geldof, seem to mostly grunt and allude to parties and the creative place they are in right now. Rock stars always look like they haven't slept for days and found their shirt rolled up under the mattress. The drummer is the only one who is articulate, but this is highly inconvenient because nobody even knows the name of the drummer in any group (unless he is Ringo). At the end of the interview they will generally meet a couple of teenage girls who won a magazine contest to meet them. The girls will just scream for five minutes. When this stops, the rock stars will again explain that they are in a creative place right now. Most likely we will never hear of this particular group ever again.

After the interview, they nearly always play the group's latest "clip". The rock song video clip is possibly the most curious form of entertainment invented so far. There are four basic rules:

1. The star must sing the song in at least seven locations over the three minutes of the recording. The locations do not need to have any relevance to the song. At least one of them should be a beach.
2. There must be attractive people dancing in at least three of the locations. These attractive people should look like they are on prohibited substances.

3. The clip must tell a story that makes absolutely no sense.
4. It is best if you have a super model who cries.

Of course, the results of this entire thing look fairly ridiculous. And you can only begin to imagine how the singer feels standing on a beach in the middle of nowhere lip-synching the song while people dance. The whole thing reminds me of one of those dreams you have after you've eaten rich Italian food.

98. Fallen Stars

For some unexplained reason celebrity writers seem genuinely surprised when famous people wear T-shirts to visit the local shop and don't look 20 when they are 65. As a result, magazines and tabloids are full of sad tales of fallen celebrities.

There is the shock-horror revelation that ageing Beatle Paul McCartney looked tired when he was up at some unholy hour pushing his baby around in the pram. Here's the scoop, people who have been up with babies all night seldom look like they are part of any type of Fab Four or fab anything for that matter.

Then there was poor old former 007 actor Timothy Dalton who was photographed wearing a T-shirt and being 58. Poor bastard. What was he thinking? The writer pointed out that he was no longer chasing evil spies or wearing sharp suits. To go and get the milk? Probably not. If he dressed as James Bond to go the shop there would certainly be more to worry about. Then he would be a washed-out eccentric who didn't know when to give up.

Celebrity magazines like to speculate about what is happening inside the homes of famous couples. The source of this information is usually unnamed "close friends". These friends seem to be able to tell what is happening in the celebrity's head. Celebrity couples apparently have a lot of fights and issue a lot of ultimatums. They also seem to have a lot of planned weddings that don't actually happen, and many break-ups and big fights with the in-laws.

Celebrities also get fat a lot. This is almost always followed by a "miracle diet" that makes them thin again, often with an interview and a book deal. The miracle diet is usually fruit, vegetables, roughage and exercise. This is accompanied by a "how to" DVD and a soft interview on one of those morning programs that begins with someone telling them how fabulous they look.

Of course, the worst pictures of celebrities are their police mugshots which are a fair bit less flattering than the air-brushed prints released by the studios. Whenever celebrities are arrested in America, the media seems to find out quickly and the mugshot is usually released to the public. Police are generally not very good photographers and often seem to enjoy the notoriety of arresting a celebrity.

In his mugshot, Nick Nolte looked like a white gorilla that had been struck by lightning. Hugh Grant looked like a naughty school boy who had been caught smoking behind the shed, and Winona Ryder resembled a bag lady who had been mugged by Mary Poppins.

99. Elvis has left the building (sort-of)

I read some time ago that, at the current rate of growth, by the year 2030 one in every four Americans will be an Elvis impersonator. This is a fairly scary thought. Elvis is a popular culture icon who died at the age of 42 in 1977 following years of over-eating and prescription drugs. Fans either want to believe his death was faked, or want to keep him alive by dressing like him and trying (often badly) to replicate his distinctive voice.

Mass Elvis impersonation was made possible by a brief period in the 1970s when Elvis grew his hair long, wore sunglasses and dressed in pyjama-style jumpsuits. This now means pretty much any human can put on a wig, buy a $5 pair of sunglasses and put some sequins on a jumpsuit and in very bad light look a bit like "The King".

You can't blame some people for believing Elvis is still alive. This long after his death Elvis still puts out about 10 new albums a year (they are all the same songs but no-one seems to notice). He still goes on tour with a group of musicians all apparently aged in their 90s (Elvis is only on the video screen but no-one seems to notice). A few years ago he put out a new song (read old song with a few musical bits added) and it went straight to the top of the charts. An album of number one hit songs also went to the top (same songs but, in fairness, in a completely different order). They also brought him back as a holograph to sing with Celine Dion. What's more, through a process of careful image manipulation, Elvis is no longer the unhappy, overweight man who died prematurely. He is younger, thinner and happier – and selling more records.

The fascination with Elvis, and perhaps to the same extent The Beatles, is nothing short of remarkable. There is still a new book every week, although it's getting harder to find new material. Upcoming titles are expected to include "Elvis once looked at me" and "I met somebody who actually met Elvis".

Then there are the song "finds". At least three times a year, a secret, previously unknown tape of Elvis or The Beatles is found in a box in the back of a studio. This raises a couple of obvious questions. How many boxes have they got back there and why don't they just check them all?

As time passes, the recording "finds" become more obscure. Within five years it will be CDs of Elvis gargling and calling his dog. This will be quickly followed by the limited extended-play remix and the UK dance version. These will all be the same but I expect no-one will notice.

100. Great trilogies

There was a time when a film director was content to make a movie, give it a decent edit and send out a final version to take its chances at the box office. The viewers were content to watch it once on the big screen, once on video, once on pay TV and every four weeks after that on free-to-air.

With the onset of DVD, that is no longer enough. We now have deleted scenes, special features, 26 hours of "previously unseen footage" and interviews with everyone from the actors to the guy who watered the plants. If you are really keen, you can watch the movie with Portuguese subtitles or with really annoying commentary from one of the 16 writers who worked on the script.

There is also the self-indulgent, dummy-spit version of the movie known as the director's cut. These are generally about 90 minutes longer than the original and include all the stuff the director shot and the film editors didn't like. Inevitably these are nowhere near as good as the original and you sit through lots of close-ups of people looking yonder, running wildlife and sunsets.

Films also come with "the making of" specials. I've always hated "making of" specials. This is where they take the magic of special effects and fantasy and tell you how they did it. It's a bit like a magician revealing he has a secret panel in his hat before he pulls the rabbit out. These are party-pooper shows. Once you have seen them, you can never really watch the movie properly.

If you like old movies, there is every chance they will eventually be released on DVD. When this happens the promoters will tell you they are even better than before because they've been "digitally remastered". I'm not really sure what digitally remastered means but it sounds fairly impressive. Curiously, the film always looks the same as the last time you saw it on TV, but you watch anyway in case any evidence of a digital remaster thing suddenly leaps on to the screen. At worst you can watch the "making of" the digital remaster or wait for the director's cut, or the documentary on the making of the director's cut.

Directors also like to keep flogging a good idea with sequels. Great sequels, like great trilogies, usually come in threes. There have been many great trilogies over the years. Some, like *Back to the Future*, are a little hard to follow without a white board. This trilogy revolves around a time machine in which a young Michael J Fox and a wild-eyed professor go back and forward in time. Everything they do in the past impacts on the future. This seems to mostly impact on photographs. If you get killed in the past you are apparently automatically wiped from future holiday snapshots. This must look fairly weird if someone has their arm around you. It is also possible that this has something to do with being digitally remastered.

Perhaps the greatest trilogy of all time is *Star Wars*. This is mostly because it was in fact two trilogies produced many years apart. *Stars Wars*, an epic tale of Jedi knights a long time ago in a galaxy far, far away, has become a culture in its own right. People dress as *Star Wars* characters, attend *Star Wars* conventions and debate *Star Wars* scenarios and scene nuances. During a recent Australian population census, thousands of people listed their religion as Jedi.

The first *Star War* trilogy began last century with a film about a boy who worked on a mysterious farm in the desert before rescuing a beautiful princess with a portable bug zapper. The boy managed to achieve this with the help of an equally mysterious old-age pensioner who lived somewhere else in the desert living off stray rodents who he hunted with a powerful weapon called the force. The force is a special power possessed only by the main stars of the film and a mysterious midget with

Tall People Don't Jump

giant ears called Yoda (the green midget is called Yoda, not the ears). Together they must fight the evil forces of the "Empire", which likes to kill people, blow up planets and generally plunder the universe.

The Empire is ruled by a man in a cloak with an annoying habit of letting it fall over his eyes, and by James Earl Jones's voice coming out of the mouth of some other guy all dressed in black.

As the trilogy unfolds, it becomes sort of clear that pretty much everyone is related or had some sort of falling out in the past. Many of them have hair problems. This is particularly so for a giant Womble called Chewbacker who seems to be made entirely of hair. The Princess also has serious hair issues with a style somewhere between a Mouseketeer and Cindy from *The Brady Bunch*.

The good guys and bad guys take turns winning. The good guys are helped by the fact that it is apparently easy to sneak onto a giant enemy starship that is sitting in the middle of space and is guarded by about a million storm troopers with nothing better to do and a giant beam that can destroy planets.

Adding to the confusion is the fact that the makers of the six-part trilogy got disoriented in the 1970s, which was not all that uncommon, and made the end of the story before they made the start. This forced them to release the conclusion before they released the beginning and to end it with the middle, leaving no room for surprise. As a result, when the "prequels" were released in the 1990s, the "shock" revelation that the once-innocent Anakin Skywalker would eventually become James Earl Jones's voice was not really that much of a shock.

Avid *Star Wars* fans, often lacking an actual life, were still very excited by the prequels and generally camped out for three days so they could be first into the theatre and see the new movie before everyone else. Of course, within 24 hours they could have seen the movie in a half-empty cinema with the extra bonus of sleep the night before.

The final movie, *Revenge of the Sith*, is particularly important because it marked the first time in decades that fans could watch the whole saga from start to finish so it all made sense. There may, of course, still be some unanswered questions. We may never know why no-one seems to have told Princess Leia about the force or given her a portable bug zapper of her own. Or for that matter why desert farm boy Luke Skywalker is the brother of the Princess but does not appear to be a prince. Or for that matter why there only seems to be about 50 good guys in the whole series. Or for that matter…

Similar questions tended to linger after the completion of the Matrix trilogy. This intriguing set of films unleashed serious arguments across the world as hapless filmgoers tried to patch together exactly what happened.

The films are dark tales in which humans do battle with machines and jump in and out of high-tech worlds full of gadgets, spaceships, robots and futuristic computer screens. In this highly-sophisticated world, the good guys battle the bad guys by kicking the crap out of each other and doing martial arts in slow motion. They move between the computer world and the real world via ordinary phone lines. This is probably uncomfortable and may result in horrendous phone bills.

The bad guys are mostly Hugo Weaving. In the early movies, there is approximately one Hugo Weaving, known as Agent Smith. By the time the third movie is in full flight, there are hundreds of Hugo Weavings, all played by Hugo Weaving. All the other actors turn into Hugo Weaving after he plunges his hand into their hearts and laughs like a maniac. This is apparently because the whole film has been infected with the Hugo Weaving virus.

Tall People Don't Jump

The hero of the tale is Nero, a brooding character with no obvious personality. Nero is the great hope of all civilisation. It is not clear why, but it seems to be important that he kicks the crap out of Hugo Weaving. Some people believe Nero is "The One". This has something to do with a prophesy that a very serious bald man keeps talking about as he looks knowingly into space. The bald man may be completely mad.

Being "The One" leads Nero to a locksmith who makes him a key that allows him to enter a door that no-one else can. This might be because they have not looked beneath the mat outside or under the pot plant. Inside the room he meets a grey-haired architect. This is very significant and may have something to do with the prophesy, the serious bald man, Hugo Weaving or perhaps someone wanting to design a building.

There is also a mysterious, elderly housewife known as the Oracle. The Oracle sees everything but won't tell anyone what she sees. After it happens, she says that was what she saw. The Oracle may be a shonk. Eventually she also becomes Hugo Weaving. Then there is the mysterious train person, a foul-tempered hippy who traps Nero in a bleak railway station. Regular city commuters can generally relate to this scene.

Meanwhile, machines are drilling through the earth trying to reach the underground city where all the humans seem to live. It is not clear if this is connected to the architect, the Oracle, the bald man, the train guy or even the rest of the movie.
At the risk of spoiling the ending for people still using a white board and scratching their heads, eventually Nero also becomes Hugo Weaving, thus fulfilling a prophesy that all actors will be Hugo Weaving.

The other great trilogy of recent times is Lord of the Rings, an epic tale of struggle, valour and jewelry envy. For more than 50 years, people have waited for the final movie in the trilogy because the book it is based on is far too long to read to the end.

The story follows the journey of a young hobbit who takes a very long walk to throw a ring into a volcano. Along the way people try to kill him.

Unless the ring is destroyed, Middle Earth will fall into the hands of the evil Sauron. Sauron is just a giant eye. We don't know much about him, but clearly nobody wants to be ruled by a giant eye.

Each instalment of the movie goes for about 18 hours, including five or six hours of battle scenes in which elves, goblins and garden gnomes take on an army of ugly *Planet of the Apes* rejects for control of an old castle in the middle of nowhere. The hero is Aragorn who is helped by Legolas, an elf who has possibly escaped from Santa's workshop at the North Pole. There is also a dwarf called Gimli who was considered too ugly for *Snow White*.

Another important character is Gandalf. Gandalf is a very tall wizard who falls into a very deep hole in the first movie but manages to kill Darth Vader and return in the second movie to help the hobbit Frodo fulfil his destiny to be a fully-fledged Jedi knight. In the first move Gandalf is known as Gandalf the Grey and dresses in grey. In the second movie he dresses in white and is known as Gandalf the, er, white. The change is apparently a good thing. It is a result of powerful magic. And Ajax.

Politics

101. The curious art of politics

Politics is perhaps the most curious of human activities. It is generally practised by over-zealous humans with a burning desire to change the world, or at least appear on television.

Budding politicians can spend many years preparing to be voted into Parliament. This begins with joining a party and can involve taking high-profile roles in local organisations, turning up at a lot of events, and buying a generous quota of Girl Guide cookies during the annual drive. Aspiring politicians can generally be easily spotted because they appear a lot in the social pages of their local newspapers and they regularly introduce themselves to total strangers.

Sometimes aspiring politicians set up roadside stalls in which they establish a desk and a chair and offer to talk to ordinary citizens about their problems. Even actually elected politicians struggle to fix problems for citizens. Aspiring politicians have absolutely no chance but people seem to appreciate them listening and giving up their weekends to sit in a folding verandah chair with a card table on the street side.

As political campaigns descend into cyberspace in search of young voters who have gone there to avoid politicians, the ancient art of political waving is making a comeback. On busy roadways across the state, morning commuters are greeted by a whole lot of party signs and then the sight of the actual human on the sign waving to them. The logic of this is that voters will see the actual human waving and say to themselves: "This actual human is waving at me. I must vote for them in the election." Sometimes the person waving is not the actual human on the political poster but a cheap stand-in wearing a T-shirt and a cap similar to the one usually worn by the candidate. In these cases, the logic is that the voter will think: "There is a person standing next to a poster waving at me. I must not vote for this person but I should vote for the person on the poster because the other person in a similar hat is waving to me." This is obviously ingenious. It says to electors: "We may not be able to help you but by golly we can wave."

102. American elections

American presidents are elected for four-year terms. American presidential election campaigns also seem to run for four years.

This means that the United States is pretty much always in election mode.

For an outsider, an American election is as difficult to follow as the country's national anthem is to sing. There are primaries, electoral colleges, state delegates and countless votes that seem to happen just about every weekend. This somehow results in the election of a single person who has the power to set off nuclear weapons.

American presidential contests are between Republicans, who believe in big business and bombing the crap out of other countries, and Democrats, who believe in big business and bombing the crap out of other countries with a slightly more compassionate expression on their faces. Before the Republicans and Democrats face each other, they have a very long-winded campaign to pick their presidential candidates. During this pre-selection process, several people from each party attack each other constantly and argue why their opponents are totally unsuitable to lead the country. Once a candidate is chosen, they all change their minds and agree that the elected candidate is the greatest person who ever walked the earth.

Somewhere in the process, the Republicans and Democrats also pick someone to run as Vice-President. This is generally considered the worst job in the country and involves a lot of photo opportunities with community groups who make cake, and kids who have won essay contests. Republicans tend to pick Vice-Presidential candidates who cannot spell potato and sometimes shoot their lawyers by accident. Every so often they will pick former beauty queens who kill moose and can attack Russia from their front lawn.

The relative worth of anyone running for office in the United States is determined by how much they look like John F Kennedy (JFK). Kennedy was an exciting young president in the 1960s who was assassinated. His brother Bobby was also assassinated while running for office. The Kennedys are the closest thing American has to royalty and everyone wants to look like them. Most media reports refer to potential candidates as JFK look-alikes, even if they are older, Afro-American women or retired Sumo wrestlers. Nobody ever questions this. Looking like a Kennedy is especially easy for actual Kennedys. There are quite a few of these, and every so often they run for office. Some of the Kennedys are actually called Kennedy. Others are hyphenated Kennedys. This generally means they are somehow related to Kennedys or married to them. The exception to this is Arnold Schwarzenegger, a former actor who was previously married to a hyphenated Kennedy and became Governor of California.

Most presidential candidates in America support family values and God. Candidates from the south also support guns. Northern candidates are more likely to support hippies and trees. Republicans always want to cut taxes. Democrats like to increase spending and put higher taxes on the rich. Republicans are the rich.

American elections are also less about policies than they are about getting young voters and minority groups to turn up at the polls in party-funded buses. The party that gets the most number of supporters to actually turn up wins the election. If lots of people turn up, the election is usually a tie and gets decided by courts in Florida. The polls are watched carefully by thousands of lawyers who sue everyone once the count is completed. When there are disputes over the count, they must be resolved by the local State Governor. The Governor is sometimes related to one of the candidates. This is regarded as democracy at work.

103. The science of spin

In modern times, it is generally accepted that anyone in politics or most aspects of public life cannot just open their mouths and say what they think. All public statements must first be spun.

Spinning is generally done by people called "spin doctors" who are paid by all manner of politicians and companies to take perfectly reasonably information and opinions and distort it in the public interest. The resulting information is not technically wrong. It is simply reconstructed to reflect a particular world view or to make the person saying it sound slightly more plausible than he otherwise would be.

Spinning is also done in politics to ensure that everyone who is a member of the same party has the same opinion. If this doesn't happen, the media will play up splits in the party and this will be seen as disunity and incohesion. Spinning allows political parties to turn bad news into good news. When the Australian Government drove the country into a prolonged recession in the early 1990s, the then Treasurer Paul Keating declared that this was in fact a good thing – it was the "recession we had to have" to combat inflation. When things were going tough for former Liberal Prime Minister Malcolm Fraser, he implied that this was situation normal because "life wasn't meant to be easy".

Most spin begins with the proposition that there is no such thing as bad news when you are in government. Everything is good news, a temporary set-back, the early stages of a long-term plan, old news that has since been dealt with, proof that the government's overall strategy is beginning to show results, or it is the other party's fault. In fact, governments can generally blame previous governments for everything that is wrong with just about everything for about five years before it starts to sound lame. After that, they blame the party in Opposition for not being supportive and talking down the economy. When this stops working, they blame unions and free radicals.

Oppositions on the other hand begin every debate with the proposition that there is no such thing as good news. Everything is bad news, too little, too late, not as good as the rest of the world, not as good as it was five years ago, proof that the government is more interested in going on world trips than running the country, likely to put the country in too much debt, not likely to be put the country in enough debt, putting our grandchildren in debt, squandering taxpayers' money or ripping off pensioners who can't afford their light bills and are being forced to live on dog food.

In the airline industry, any "incident" needs to be aggressively spun to avoid an avalanche of people refusing the fly. Hence, when a hole blows out in the side of a plane or part of the wing falls off, a spokesperson usually writes these off as "minor incidents that are part of the normal operation of an airline". After plane crashes, which are quite rare, airlines like to point out that they are still safer than other forms of transport, like rocket-powered motorcycles and stunt cannons.

When companies recall products for safety reasons, the spin always suggests that there is no actual danger; the company was merely blowing $400 million to make absolutely sure that the product was absolutely safe. They seldom mention that lawyers have advised them they had better do the recall before they got sued for billions of dollars and put out of business.

The origins of spin can be found in advertising, where salespeople have for years been trying for new and more creative ways to make boring products sound interesting and in need of urgent purchase. Often they use famous or beautiful people to deliver the spin on the basis that, if famous and beautiful people believe it, then it must be important, or at least successful enough to afford a famous or beautiful person to flog it. Advertising likes to suggest that people are running out of time to act. Everything is for a limited time, with limited supplies and only while stocks last. People are urged to get in early so they won't be disappointed. Advertising spin people really hate disappointment.

Finishing the story

104. The end (almost)

It is well accepted in story-telling circles that any flog can start a story and keep it going. The skill comes in finishing it.

Some television series have gone on for decades apparently because no-one could think of a way to end them.

The writers of *Friends were* apparently involved in countless meetings to come up with an ending. *Gilligan's Island* was axed before it could be ended. As someone pointed out, this was a show where the Professor could make a radio out of a coconut but couldn't fix a hole in the boat. No wonder they couldn't finish it.

Other times they finish them in bizarre fashion. In the 1970s Australian soap opera *Number 96,* they just herded the whole cast into a room and blew them up. In *Seinfeld,* they sent the cast to jail. In M*A*S*H, Hawkeye went mad and started yabbering about a chook.

Throughout history, writers have struggled to end their stories. As a result, about one in every three stories ends with the phrase "only time will tell". Fairy tale writers didn't have a clue how to finish up, so they ended everything with "they all lived happily ever after". Nobody actually believed this. Cinderella and that prince, for example, based their whole relationship on a shoe. I doubt that would have worked.

Equally, no-one believes Jack turned out okay after he exchanged a cow for some beans, stole a goose and chopped down a beanstalk. By the time he was 20, that boy was going to be bankrupt and in jail for theft, assault and vandalism.

In the 1970s, movie-makers faced with an inability to finish their stories resorted to really weird or unhappy endings. This reached its ridiculous crescendo in a movie called *Earthquake* when Charlton Heston survived continental shift, fires, bursting dams and bad acting only to dive into some fairly tame flowing water to save a woman he didn't like. As a result, he drowned. This left an entire generation depressed and drove them to flairs, tight pants and disco music.

When the Bruce Willis movie *The Sixth Sense* came out with a shock ending, everyone was, well, shocked. It also left them traumatised. After years of bad endings, no endings and endings that came before the beginnings (as in *Star Wars*), no-one was ready for a surprise ending. Some were so affected they started seeing dead people.

Many writers have just thrown their arms in the air and said: "I can't end the bloody thing, end it yourself". This sentiment has ushered in the alternative-ending genre. If you don't like the ending they give you, they have others.

Over recent years we have sat through the television series *24*. This is based on the lucky number 24. It went for 24 hours based on 24 episodes of an hour each. After investing so much time and energy in this show, the ending in season one was a total dud. The makers knew this and immediately put on an advertisement for the *24* DVD which has a different ending. I haven't seen it but I expect a narrator who sounds like Walt Disney just comes on and declares: "They all lived happily ever after".

In the future, *24* may well come back as *23*, after Jack Bauer negotiates a lunch hour.

If you do not like this ending, please write your own.

The End (for real)

ABOUT THE AUTHOR

Shane Rodgers is a writer, business executive, marketer and communicator with an intense curiosity about what makes people tick. As a journalist he covered social issues, politics, statistics, popular culture, police, courts, education, mining and rural issues. He was a columnist for *The Courier-Mail* in the 1990s and wrote the satirical Paradox column in the now defunct *City News* publication in Brisbane and the Thirsty Cow column for the APN regional media group. Shane lives in the Australian city of Brisbane.

Printed in Great Britain
by Amazon